WHO'S AFRAID OF
INDIAN COOKING?

(A BOOK OF MENUS)

WHO'S AFRAID OF INDIAN COOKING?

(A BOOK OF MENUS)

LALI NAYAR
RAJUL SUXENA

UBSPD
UBS Publishers' Distributors Ltd.
New Delhi Bombay Bangalore Madras
Calcutta Patna Kanpur London

UBS Publishers' Distributors Ltd.
5 Ansari Road, New Delhi 110002
Bombay, Bangalore, Madras
Calcutta, Patna, Kanpur, London

First Published 1994

ISBN 81-86112-64-2

Cover Design : UBS ART Studio
Cover Photo : Michael Tyson
Inside Photos : Pradeep Dasgupta/Fotomedia

Lasertypeset in 11pt. Futura at Folio, G-68, Connaught Circus, N. Delhi-110 001
Printed at Rajkamal Electric Press B 35/9 G T Karnal Road, Delhi 110 033

TO OUR HUSBANDS AND CHILDREN
WHO HAVE ENCOURAGED US ALL ALONG
TO WRITE THIS BOOK.
THEIR WORDS
"YOU CAN DO IT"
HAS ITS RESULTS!

CONTENTS

CELEBRATION DINNER FOR NON-VEGETARIANS (MENU)

SPECIAL OCCASION VEGETARIAN BUFFET (MENU)

AN INVITATION TO INDIAN COOKING

With Pizza Huts in Delhi, McDonalds in Moscow, and Fish and Chips bars in Japan, peoples' attitudes towards food have changed. The change seems here to stay and does make things interesting—so why not? Variety is truly now the spice of life, and within this context Indian food with its uncanny charm has really found its own niche.

The gradual awakening of interest in Indian cuisine is reflected in the worldwide mushrooming of the Indian food business. Not so long ago Indian food was considered 'strange' and 'mysterious', but now it is not at all uncommon to hear all over the world "Oh, we are having curry tonight!"

A few adventurous cooks might try their hand at making some Indian food at home, but for a large number, a quick trip to the Indian restaurant around the corner might just suffice. No doubt, many of these restaurants do provide a high standard of food with different interpretations of what eating in India is all about. A few such outings, possibly combined with accepting hospitality from many an Indian home has generated a further interest in the exploration of Indian cuisine.

However, we feel that no matter what rating any of these Indian restaurants might achieve, there is nothing to beat real home cooking! Many people would like to recreate at home the food they have enjoyed outside and even though they can find plenty of recipes around, selecting a few to plan a proper meal for various occasions is generally a problem. Keeping this in mind we have assembled some menus ranging from the very simple to the more elaborate. These menus will provide invaluable help in recreating typical Indian meals to suit all occasions.

Although there is an incredible variety of menus within Indian cuisine, we have selected what we think are the tastiest, the most typical, and the ones used in some form or the other in every Indian home, rich or poor. All the menus are tried and tested, accurately described and easy to follow. We have included for your convenience, special features such as advance preparation, useful hints, and tips for freezing. All these will help to transform an ordinary cook into a distinguished one.

1

Being busy housewives ourselves, we are fully aware of the constraints of time due to the pace of modern life. We, have therefore, slightly adapted some of our recipes accordingly, without of course, sacrificing their authenticity.

Indian food has got not only tremendous potential for providing the ideal combination of taste and flavour but, is relatively economical and above all wholesome and nutritious as well. The West is at last recognizing the emphasis it lays on the use of cereals, pulses, vegetables etc., which as we all know leads to a well balanced diet; therefore, the impression held by many, that Indian food is fattening is not entirely correct.

We feel that depending upon your choice of dishes within the vast range available, it is quite easy to pick a number of dishes which are low in fat content and therefore ideal for those watching their weight. Bearing this in mind, we have included a section on diet menus both for vegetarians and non-vegetarians. We hope this section of diet menus will be particularly useful for those whose love of Indian food surpasses their weight consciousness and be also beneficial for many a weight-watcher, who although new to the world of Indian cuisine, might be seeking that 'different diet plan'.

Our aim has been to provide at a glance, a handy collection of readymade menus to suit every mood and occasion, be it an informal lunch, a tea party, a barbecue, an elaborate dinner or simply filling a lunch box. This book will give you the confidence to cook 'Indian style' with ease—so much so that in time, you might hear yourself say, 'Who's afraid of Indian cooking? Not me!'

SECRETS OF SUCCESS

Surely cooking should be a pleasure and not a chore! If you are an absolute beginner, it is natural to be a little apprehensive, but by keeping in mind a few suggestions given in this book, you will help yourself to feel 'in-charge' and look forward to your 'trials'. We hope that even the more experienced cook might gain some new ideas and inspiration from us.

The beauty of Indian cooking lies in its flexibility which allows one the freedom to vary the ingredients and their proportions (especially the spices) to suit one's own palate. Once you have grasped the basics, it is easy to make changes, but we recommend that initially at least, the recipes should be followed as closely as possible. Try not to be tempted to cut corners in the preparation or cooking procedures as you will find that in the end it has probably not been worth it.

Before commencing the actual cooking, it is important to read through the entire recipe carefully. Our experience with Indian cooking teaches us that often there is very little time in between the various stages of the cooking procedure (sometimes merely a few seconds) therefore it is essential to assemble all required ingredients and equipment and keep it ready at hand. This will not only avoid last minute panic but also ensure a smooth and continuous work flow.

Planning the meal and choosing the various dishes always needs some thought, or one might end up with a table-full of dishes, all of which look and taste the same. The selection of an appropriate menu, therefore, becomes highly relevant to ensure the success of any meal. We have already done this ground work for you by putting together a combination of recipes and have compiled appropriate menus which include variety in taste, flavour, texture and colour. We are certain that as you gain confidence, you will readily be able to interchange these recipes and create your own special, personalized menus.

3

SPECIAL TECHNIQUES AND INGREDIENTS

MASALA

The word *masala* is a wide-ranging term, which simply means a mixture of dry spice powders or the combination of several ingredients as diverse as onions, ginger, garlic, natural yoghurt, tomatoes, whole spices, ground spices, herbs etc. When some or all of the said ingredients are used in a certain proportion and fried or roasted to a certain stage and consistency, they are then called a *masala*. It certainly does not have a single mode of preparation but may be prepared in various ways. Nevertheless each method produces its own distinctive taste and flavour.

This *masala* lies at the very heart of successful curry making. The skill and judgment in preparing a good *masala*, more than anything else, determines the final results.

Here are some useful tips to remember while preparing a 'rich' *masala*.

a. Use a heavy-based pan.

b. Heat ghee/oil and fry onions till golden brown (remember the taste and appearance of a dish can alter if the onions turn too dark a colour).

c. Add ingredients in the same order as given in the recipe.

d. As many of the ingredients will easily stick to the bottom of the pan, it is essential to watch over them whilst frying—scraping and stirring continually.

e. Tomatoes, when used should be skinned and finely chopped. Natural yoghurt should always be gently beaten and added a little at a time, in order to blend into a homogeneous mixture.

f. A slight change in the aroma and the separation of ghee/oil from the hot mixture are sure signs of the *masala* being done.

BAGHAR

Baghar means seasoning with various spices or other ingredients cooked in hot ghee/oil. Depending on the dish being prepared, this seasoning may either be the first step in preparing a dish or the last one.

In the first instance e.g., as in Baghare Chawal, the seasoning flavours the ghee/oil and is then further cooked along with the rest of the ingredients, bringing out all the dormant flavours of the various spices used. When the seasoning is done towards the end, e.g., as in Tadke Wali Daal, it helps to give a fresh flavour and enhances the aroma of the completed dish. Detailed instructions for various seasonings are given in the recipes where required.

GINGER AND GARLIC PUREE/PASTE

Many of the recipes in this book call for the use of ginger and garlic. To peel and chop these every time they are needed is somewhat tedious, especially when they are required in very small quantities! However, it is always useful if sufficient amounts of ginger and garlic are prepared in advance and kept. This will keep for weeks when stored in an air-tight container in the fridge and can save you a lot of time and trouble, especially when you are in a rush.

Either puree ginger and garlic separately or combine the two together to keep ready at hand.

GINGER PUREE

10 oz (275g) ginger; 2-3 tablespoons water.
Scrape ginger and chop roughly. Place in a liquidizer along with the water and work to a smooth puree. (And a little more water if needed.)

Remove and store in an airtight container in the fridge.
Note: $1/2$" (1.25cm) ginger is roughly equivalent to 1 tsp (5 ml) ginger puree.

GARLIC PUREE

6 oz (175 g) garlic
2 tablespoons water
Peel garlic and follow above method.

GINGER-GARLIC PUREE

GARAM MASALA

GHEE

Note: 2 fat cloves of garlic are roughly equivalent to 1 tsp (5 ml) garlic puree.

10 oz (275 g) ginger
6 oz (175 g) garlic
4-5 tablespoons (60-75 ml) water

Peel and scrape ginger and garlic and follow the above method to grind them.

The word *garam* means hot and *masala* means a specified mixture of spices. Although commercially prepared *garam masala* is readily available, we think it is well worth making one's own as this will most certainly have a better flavour. *Garam masala* is a highly aromatic combination of spices which really has no set formula, as it can be made in a wide variety of combinations. The spices used should always be whole and only small quantities should be made at any given time in order to retain their full flavour and freshness. Here is one of our favourite combinations of ingredients for *garam masala*.

3/4 oz (20 g) brown cardamoms
3/4 oz (20 g) cinnamon
1/4 oz (7 g) black cumin seeds
1/4 oz (7 g) cloves
10 black peppercorns
large pinch grated nutmeg

Shell the cardamoms and grind along with the rest of the ingredients to a fine powder. Store immediately in an airtight container. It will keep well provided the lid is replaced immediately after use.

A variety of vegetable cooking oils are used in Indian preparations but *ghee*, which is simply clarified butter remains a favourite. It has a flavour all its own and is unique as a cooking medium. Although its calorie content is higher than most of the other vegetable oils, relatively smaller amounts of ghee are required for cooking. It is easily available in Indian grocery stores and now in many large supermarkets as well. If you are feeling enthusiastic and want to make *ghee* at home (which many Indian housewives do) here is an easy method:

You will need

8 oz (225 g) unsalted butter; a heavy-based pan
Melt the butter on medium heat, stirring frequently. Reduce heat to very low and simmer gently till the entire water content dries up and the solid residue settles to the bottom. It is important to stir occasionally to prevent the residue from burning, otherwise it will impart an undesirable flavour. Cool, but do not stir; decant the liquid *(ghee)* and strain it through a piece of muslin. Store in a jar with a tight-fitting lid. It will keep for 2 to 3 months.

PANEER

Paneer is home-made Indian cheese widely used in making sweetmeats and vegetarian dishes. It is surprisingly easy to make at home, requiring no great ingenuity or special equipment. It is a versatile ingredient which adds that special touch to many a recipe. In India it is always freshly made and used, but it can be easily prepared ahead of time and deep frozen. It freezes beautifully, specially so, if fried and kept.

To make *paneer* (Approximately 4-6 oz i.e., 100-175 g)

You will need

1 pint (20 fl oz) full cream milk; 1 tablespoon lime juice mixed in 1 cup hot water
or $^1/_2$ tsp citric acid mixed in 1 cup hot water

Boil milk for 4 to 5 minutes, reduce heat and gradually add a cup of hot water either with lime juice or with citric acid. Stir gently once or twice while adding the hot water. Remove from heat and leave it covered for about 15 minutes or so till all the milk curdles. Strain through a muslin cloth and squeeze out all the whey. The milk solids left in the bag is *paneer*.

If cubes of *paneer* are required, then leave *paneer* in the same bag and press it down with a heavy weight for 2 to 3 hours to form a slab. Cut into even-sized pieces and fry till golden brown if required e.g., as in palak paneer.

TOFU

Although a poor substitute for paneer (whose taste and flavour are hard to match), in case you have no alternative we suggest you use tofu. Tofu is soya bean curd which looks like paneer and comes in readymade slabs which can be found in supermarkets.

NATURAL YOGHURT (CURDS)

The value of natural yoghurt has been recognized in the East since ancient times. Undoubtedly a versatile ingredient, natural yoghurt (unsweetened) finds many uses in Indian cooking—be it to enrich dishes, impart a creamy texture, or thicken curries. It may be used as a tenderizer in marinades, or just simply be eaten on its own. Follow the simple method given below to make it.

To make natural yoghurt at home

You will need
1 pint (600 ml) milk
1 tbsp live natural yoghurt (for best results whole milk thick set natural yoghurt is recommended)

Boil the milk for 4 to 5 minutes and then allow it to cool to blood heat or body temperature i.e., about 38°C. Add the beaten yoghurt and blend it in thoroughly using a whisk. Cover and leave it undisturbed in a warm place for several hours.

In hot weather the yoghurt will set in about 4-5 hours; but in cooler climates, it is best to wrap the container in a warm blanket and leave it undisturbed fo 8-10 hours or overnight in a warm place. Once the yoghurt is set, transfer it to the fridge to prevent it from getting too sharp. Fresh home-made yoghurt is extremely palatable with a mild, refreshing taste. It will easily keep for several days in the fridge.

COMMON TERMS USED IN INDIAN COOKERY

ACHAAR (PICKLE)

Any kind of fruit, vegetable, meat or fish can be preserved. Pickles are usually spicy, hot and sour. Mango pickle is one of the most popular pickles.

BHAJI (COOKED DRY VEGETABLE)

Bhajis are much quicker and simpler to prepare as compared with khormas and koftas.

BHARTA (ROASTED, MASHED VEGETABLE)

One of the many different ways of preparing vegetables. These are usually roasted, mashed and lightly seasoned.

BAGHAR (TADKA)

Sizzling hot, oil-based seasoning/tempering or dressing. A unique method of seasoning/dressing, used to bring out the dormant flavours of various whole spices, onions, garlic etc., by frying them in hot oil/ghee. This hot mixture or *baghar* is poured over the cooked dish to give the final finishing touch. Alternatively it can be the initial stage in the preparation of a dish, so that the flavours are incorporated during the cooking process.

BHUNA (ADJECTIVE) (PAN-FRIED, DRY)

Dry or almost dry meat or vegetable dish.

BHARWAN (STUFFED DISH)

Another popular way of preparing vegetables which may be stuffed with a variety of ingredients.

DAHI

(Natural yoghurt) An extremely useful and versatile ingredient which finds endless uses in Indian cooking (See page 8).

DHULI

(Washed) Lentils are often washed and their skins removed.

DUM	(Pot-roasting) This technique of slow cooking in steam (using a tight-fitting lid) at the final stage, not only tenderizes the ingredients, but also enhances the flavour and appearance by drying off the surplus liquid and gently bringing the oil/ghee to the surface.
GOSHTH	(Meat)
HALWA	(Sweetmeat) Served both as a snack or pudding, the most popular being the carrot or semolina *halwa*. Generally on the richer side but irresistible.
KHOYA	(Dried fresh whole milk) Traditionally an important ingredient in the preparation of many Indian sweetmeats. Sometimes also used in rich non-vegetarian preparations.
KHORMA	(Rich mild curry) A special type of meat or vegetable curry enriched with cream, yoghurt, nuts and spices— usually on the mild side.
KABAB	(Roasted/fried spicy meats) A distinctive method of preparing meats, fish and poultry served mainly as snacks or part of a full meal.
KULFI	(Indian ice-cream) A very rich and scrumptious ice-cream prepared by an age-old traditional Indian method.
MAKHANI	(Buttery) Butter imparts a distinctive flavour to the dish.
MASALA	(Mixture of spices). (See Page 4)
PANEER	(Indian cream cheese). (See Page 7)
TOFU (SOYA BEAN CURD)	A rich source of vegetable protein used extensively in Far Eastern countries and an easy and ideal alternative to home-made paneer. It does not have any particular flavour of its own but has a tremendous capacity to absorb the flavour of added ingredients.

SAADA	(Plain) Basic or simple.
SAABUT	(Whole).
SABZI	(Vegetables).
SHARBAT (SWEETENED COOL DRINK)	Traditional Indian cool drink made with sugar and extracts of one or more of the following: fruits/flowers/nuts/herbs. Sharbats are very refreshing and effective coolants during summer.
TANDOORI (CLAY-OVEN BAKING)	A very special and ancient method of cooking in a clay oven (tandoor). Tandoori dishes are well-known and a great favourite amongst connoisseurs.
TARKARI	(Vegetable)
TAZA	(Fresh)
TALNA	(Deep fry)
TIKKA	(Pieces of marinated and grilled meat) somewhat similar to kababs.
VINDALOO (NONE)	Hot and spicy dish using vinegar-based masala.

KITCHEN EQUIPMENT AND ALTERNATIVES

The utensils generally found in any average kitchen would no doubt suffice for all Indian cooking. However, the traditional equipment as used in Indian kitchens are mentioned below together with suitable and modern alternatives.

KADHAI

A deep and semi-circular pan with handles. It is usually made of cast iron or stainless steel and should ideally have a heavy base. Useful for deep frying as it requires less oil while providing a large surface area for frying.

TAVA

A flat and slightly concave, thick, cast iron griddle, approximately 10" (25.5 cm) in diameter with or without handles. Used for making Indian breads.

CHAKLA BELAN

The *chakla* is a round disc about 10" (25.5 cm) in diameter made from marble/stone/wood which stands on three short legs. The *belan* is a slimmer version of the standard Western rolling pin. Used for rolling Indian breads like *chappatis*, *parathas* etc., any available rolling pin and pastry board/work surface will do equally well.

MASALA DABBA

A spice-box with a tight-fitting lid. Usually made of stainless steel and round in shape, it has 6-7 small containers fitted inside it. Extremely handy for keeping an assortment of frequently used spices e.g., turmeric, chilli, salt, cumin, coriander and mustard seeds etc., within easy reach of the cook.

SALAAKH/SEEKH	Basically like skewers, they are thick (approximately $\frac{1}{4}$" i.e. 0.5 cm) and rectangular in cross-section. Used for making *seekh kababs* and *chicken tikkas* etc. Alternatively, use the thickest barbecue skewers you can find.
PATILA/BHAGONA	Generally heavy-based pots and pans with fitting lids. The heavy base helps in even frying and prevents ingredients from sticking and burning while cooking. Tight-fitting lids are essential, especially for cooking rice and curries etc.
IMAMDASTA	A pestle and mortar, ideal for grinding very small quantities of whole spices e.g., green cardamoms, saffron, etc.
CHIMTA	Tongs which save fingers from burning! They are especially handy when making *chappatis* and roasting *paapads* etc.
CHANNI	A sieve or strainer.
KADHCHUL/PONI	A long handled, stainless steel, slotted spoon usually round and flattened. Invaluable for frying purposes although an ordinary slotted spoon will do as well.
KADDU-KUS	A hand grater.
KULFI-KE-SANCHE	Cone-shaped aluminium/plastic moulds, about 3-4" (7.5-10 cm) long, used for freezing *kulfi* (Indian ice-cream).
	Alternatively use any ice-cream mould/tray.
MALMAL KA TUKDA	A piece of muslin cloth approximately 18" x 18" (45 x 45 cm) used for straining purposes.
SIL-BATTA	This is the traditional all purpose grinding stone which grinds anything from dry to wet ingredients. To save

time and elbow grease, use a food processor/liquidizer/grinder.

PRESSURE COOKER

A relatively recent addition, it is widely used and is invaluable in cutting down cooking time (especially for lentils and meats) as well as retaining more food value.

CUP EQUIVALENTS			
Measure	Rice/Daal etc.	Flour	Milk/water etc.
1 cup	200 g	100 g	200 mla

Informal Lunch for Vegetarians

TADKE WALI DAAL
Seasoned Red Lentils

BAINGAN KA BHARTA
Roasted Aubergines

CHAPPATI
Wholemeal Unleavened Bread

KACHUMBER
*Tomato, Cucumber and Onion
Salad*

KHEER
Rice Pudding

Serves four to six people

Tadke Wali Daal
seasoned red lentils

Pulses form an integral part of every Indian meal. They are delicious, nutritious, and economical too.

Indians firmly believe that certain spices used in seasoning the pulses not only improve their taste but also help to make them more easily digestible. This recipe comes from the Northern and Central parts of the country.

You Will Need

8 oz (225 g) split red lentils

1³/₄ pints (1litre) water

¹/₂ tsp turmeric powder

¹/₄ tsp red chilli powder

1 tsp salt, or to taste

2 tbsp ghee or vegetable oil

1 tsp white cumin seeds

1-2 whole red or green chillies (optional)

2 oz (60 g) onions, peeled and finely chopped

1-2 medium sized tomatoes, chopped

2 tbsp ghee or vegetable oil

1 tbsp fresh green coriander leaves, finely chopped

1 tbsp butter (optional)

Remove any grit, if present, and wash lentils in 3 or 4 changes of water. Place the lentils, in the measured amount of water, turmeric and chilli powders in a heavy-based saucepan and bring to a boil. Reduce heat, partially cover pan and allow contents to simmer for approximately 15-20 minutes, or until lentils are tender.

Add salt and mix well—if too dry, add a little more (boiled) water to obtain a creamy consistency. Remove pan from heat and keep aside.

For the tempering
Heat ghee or cooking oil in a small saucepan and when hot, add cumin seeds and whole chillies (optional). When the seeds begin to sizzle, add the chopped onions and fry till light brown. Then add chopped tomatoes and cook for 2-3 minutes.

Pour this hot seasoning over the cooked lentils and cover pan immediately to allow flavours to infuse. Serve hot, sprinkled with fresh green coriander leaves and dotted with butter (optional).

Handy Hints
1. To improve the appearance of this dish, turn out the cooked lentils (prior to tempering) in a serving

Contd. ....

bowl and add the hot seasoning on top. Do not mix, but cover immediately.

2. If desired, the juice of half a fresh lemon may be sprinkled on the daal along with the fresh coriander leaves; or serve the daal with wedges of fresh lime/lemon on the side.

BAINGAN KA BHARTA
roasted aubergines

YOU WILL NEED

1 lb (450 g) aubergines

1 tsp vegetable cooking oil

3 tbsp ghee

4 oz (115 g) onions, peeled and sliced

2 green chillies, sliced (optional)

1 tsp fresh ginger, peeled and shredded

1 tsp salt, or to taste

1/4 tsp red chilli powder

4 oz (100 g) tomatoes, skinned and chopped

1 tsp garam masala powder

Baingan ka bharta is a firm favourite from Northern India and falls into a class all its own. The word bharta means to mash. When making this dish, the aubergines (brinjals) are traditionally roasted over an open charcoal fire—which imparts to them a wonderful barbecued aroma, and then mashed. The larger variety of aubergines, which have fewer seeds, are best suited for this unusual dish.

Grease the aubergines lightly with the vegetable cooking oil and roast them over a gas ring or under a pre-heated grill, turning them occasionally until they are soft and the skin is charred. Cool and remove the burnt skin. Flake off the flesh with a fork and keep aside.

Heat the ghee in a large frying pan and gently saute the onions for 2-3 minutes. Add ginger and green chillies and fry for a further minute or so. Then add the salt, red chilli powder and the chopped tomatoes. Mix well and cook until the tomatoes are softened. Now add the flaked aubergines, stir gently, cover and cook on low heat for approximately 5-7 minutes. Remove from heat, sprinkle garam masala powder and serve hot.

Handy Hints
1. To increase the quantity of this dish slightly, add 4 oz (100 g) of fresh green peas along with the tomatoes.

2. For added flavour, spike the greased aubergines (by making small insertions with a sharp knife) with 4-5 peeled cloves of garlic and 3-4 green chillies, prior to roasting them.

Chutney & Achaar

Paneer Matar, Naan

Seekh Kabab

Naan, Paratha, Misi Roti

Navratan Biryani

Aloo & Palak

Tali Machli

CHAPPATI
wholemeal unleavened bread

You Will Need

8 oz (225 g) whole-wheat flour

1/3 pint (200 ml) water, approximately

2 oz (60 g) whole-wheat flour for rolling out

1 oz (30 g) melted ghee or butter (optional)

Chappati is one of the simplest forms of unleavened Indian breads, of which there is a very wide selection.

Chappatis are made from whole wheat flour, known as atta. Although they may be made in advance and kept, they taste much better if served as soon as possible after preparation.

Special Requirements
Heavy cast iron frying pan or griddle, pair of tongs, rolling pin, and pastry board.

For the dough
Sieve the flour into a large mixing bowl, and add sufficient water to form a soft (but not sticky) dough. Knead it very thoroughly to make it pliable. Cover, and leave it to rest for 15 minutes.

For the chappati
Divide the dough into 12 portions and shape each into a round ball. Place it on a floured pastry board, flatten and roll it out with the help of a little dry flour into a thin pancake-like shape about 6" (15 cm) in diameter.

Heat the griddle on a medium flame, and when hot, transfer rolled out chappati on to the griddle. After a few seconds, as soon as small bubbles appear on the surface, turn the chappati over with the help of the tongs. Cook briefly till a few brown specks appear on the underside. Turn chappati over and press lightly around the edges with a clean, folded piece of cloth, till it starts to swell in the middle.

Remove from the hot griddle, and apply a little ghee

Contd. ....

or butter over one side. Cook all the chappatis in this way and serve immediately.

This dough makes 12 normal-size chappatis.

Handy Hints

1. If chappatis are made in advance, they should be placed one above the other, wrapped up in a clean tea towel, and stored in a tightly covered container.

2. Chappatis may also be frozen, interleaved with grease-proof paper and covered in aluminium foil. They can be re-heated in a medium oven, whilst still in the foil.

KACHUMBER
tomato, cucumber and onion salad

Salads add variety to any meal, and this one is simplicity itself. It consists of a mixture of raw vegetables with contrasting flavours and textures. Unlike Western salads, the dressing is kept to a bare minimum, and frequently omitted altogether.

You Will Need

8 oz (225 g) cucumber

6 oz (180 g) tomatoes

2 oz (60 g) onions

$^1/_2$ tsp salt

$^1/_4$ tsp freshly ground black pepper

1 tbsp lemon juice

Dice the cucumber and tomatoes and chop onions finely. Place them in a serving bowl and add salt, freshly ground black pepper and lemon juice. Mix gently. Chill lightly and serve.

KHEER
rice pudding

YOU WILL NEED

2 pints (1.2 litres) full fat milk

2 oz (60 g) rice

2 tsp ghee

6 oz (180 g) sugar, or to taste

4 green cardamoms, 2 cardamoms shelled and seeds powdered

10-12 blanched, shredded almonds (optional)

2 tsp sultanas (optional)

1 tsp rose water

Basic rice pudding is perhaps one of the simplest of desserts, but it can so easily be transformed into something special by the addition of almonds, cashew and pistachio sultanas, saffron, silver leaves etc. This is a simple version of the dish.

Soak rice in a cup of water for 20-25 minutes. Drain and coarsely crush grains of rice. Bring milk to boil and keep it simmering.

In a large saucepan, heat ghee and add 2 whole green cardamoms. After a few seconds, add the drained rice. Stir and fry for a few seconds until the grains are well coated—but do not let them brown.

Pour the hot milk over the rice, stir and mix well. Allow to cook slowly over a low flame for an hour or so, stirring frequently until the mixture has thickened and reduced by about a third at least, or more.

Add sugar and sultanas (optional). Stir to mix and continue to cook further until all the sugar has dissolved and a creamy consistency is obtained. Keep stirring the kheer often to prevent the mixture from sticking to the bottom of the pan.

Remove from heat. Allow to cool, and add powdered cardamom, rose water and mix well.

Decorate with shredded almonds (optional). Serve hot or cold.

Informal Lunch for Non-Vegetarians

TAMATAR WALI MACHLI
Tomato Fish Curry

CHAUNKI HUI HARI MATAR
Seasoned Green Peas

SADE UBLE CHAWAL
Plain Boiled Rice

KHEERE AUR MOOLI KA SALAAD
Cucumber and Radish Salad

MAZEDAR KELA
Banana Surprise

Serves four to six people

TAMATAR WALI MACHLI
tomato fish curry

YOU WILL NEED

1 lb (450 g) cod steaks

any non-oily firm-fleshed white fish or halibut cut into 2 x 3" (5 cm x 8 cm) pieces

2 tsp lemon juice for rubbing over the fish

1 tsp salt, or to taste

4 tbsp melted ghee or vegetable cooking oil

8-10 tbsp button onions, skinned but left whole

$1/_4$ tsp red chilli powder, or to taste

FOR THE SAUCE

2 tbsp vegetable cooking oil

2 oz (60 g) onions, peeled and grated

2 cloves garlic, peeled and crushed

1 lb (450 g) ripe tomatoes, skinned and chopped

India has numerous rivers and a very large coastline which provide her with an abundance of fish. For people living in the coastal regions, fish is an important part of their staple diet. Both fried and curried fish are popular—the latter is mostly accompanied by plain boiled rice.

To prepare the fish
Rub lemon juice and salt over the fish pieces and keep aside for 10-15 minutes.

Heat ghee/cooking oil and fry the button onions lightly, remove and keep them aside. To the same ghee add the fish pieces and red chilli powder and allow to cook on low heat for a few minutes, until the fish is almost though not fully cooked. Remove the fish and keep aside.

To prepare the sauce
Heat the oil and saute the onions and garlic gently. Add the tomatoes and salt and cook for 15-20 minutes on medium heat until onions are soft.

Pass the above mixture through a sieve. Return it to heat and add red chilli powder, sugar, tomato colouring and water. Stir and simmer for several minutes until the sauce thickens.

Pour the sauce over the prepared fish (placed in a deep frying pan) along with the sliced capsicums, sliced ginger and button onions. Simmer on very low heat until the fish is cooked. Serve hot, garnished with chopped mint leaves and tomato wedges.

24

Contd. ....

1 tsp salt, or to taste

$1/_2$ tsp red chilli powder

1 desp sugar

$1/_4$ tsp red food colouring

2 fl oz (60 ml) water

2 oz (55 g) capsicums,
sliced (or 3 green chillies
for a hotter dish)

For Garnish

1 medium sized tomato cut
into wedges

1 tsp fresh mint leaves, cut
finely

Handy Hints

1. Do not use green chillies if a milder taste is
   required.

2. This dish can easily be adapted for vegetarians
   by using paneer/tofu (see page 9 and 10)
   instead of fish.

CHAUNKI HUI HARI MATAR
seasoned green peas

This dish is exceptionally quick and easy to prepare. It is best made using fresh, tender green peas, but frozen ones will give almost equally good results.

YOU WILL NEED

1 tbsp vegetable cooking oil or ghee

1 tsp cumin seeds

1 clove garlic, peeled and finely minced

1-2 green chillies, finely sliced

1 lb (450 g) shelled green peas

1 tsp salt, or to taste

$1/4$ tsp red chilli powder

1 tsp lime or lemon juice, preferably freshly squeezed

1 tbsp fresh green coriander leaves, finely chopped

4 tbsp water

Heat ghee/cooking oil in a saute pan or deep frying pan and when hot add the cumin seeds. When these begin to sizzle add the garlic and green chillies. Stir for a few seconds but do not let the latter brown. Immediately add the peas, salt and red chilli powder. Stir and fry for 1 or 2 minutes. Mix well, add water and then cover the pan and cook on medium heat until the peas are just tender. If necessary sprinkle a little more water. Do not overcook.

Turn off the heat, sprinkle the lime/lemon juice and half of the green coriander. Mix gently, and if any liquid remains, return to heat, uncover pan and cook until all the liquid is absorbed.

Serve hot, garnished with the remaining coriander leaves.

Handy Hint

If desired, add one or two medium-sized boiled potatoes cut into $1/2$" (1.25 cm) cubes along with the peas. If frozen peas are used there is no need to add water. For best results use a tender and sweet variety of peas.

Sade Uble Chawal
plain boiled rice

You Will Need

12 oz (340 g) Basmati rice

18 fl oz (540 ml) water

Of all the different varieties of rice available, Basmati is generally acknowledged as the King of Rice. Its slender, long grains have a delicate and pleasant aroma. The name Basmati itself literally means the fragrant one. When cooked, this rice remains fluffy and separate and does not ·become soggy or sticky due to its low starch content.

Clean and wash the rice in several changes of water until the water runs clear.

Drain the rice through a sieve and then soak it in the measured amount of water, leaving it to stand for 15-20 minutes.

Put the rice together with the water in which it has been soaking into a large, heavy-based pan. (Remember the cooked rice will increase in volume by two to three times.) Bring it to a boil, stir gently once, and cover the pan with a tight-fitting lid. Reduce the heat to very low and allow the rice to cook undisturbed for 10-12 minutes.

Remove the pan from heat but do not open the lid for a further 5 minutes. Serve warm as cold rice loses some of its flavour.

Handy Hints

1. If using a pressure cooker: Take equal amounts (by weight) of rice and water. Pressure cook by bringing the pressure to 15 lbs on high heat. Leave for a minute or two, then remove the pressure cooker from heat and allow the pressure to drop by itself.

2. If using a microwave : Take equal amounts of rice

Contd. ....

and water and put in a fairly large microwave bowl with a lid. Cook on the highest power for 5 minutes. Remove lid, stir rice gently, cover and cook for a further 5 minutes. Let the rice stand for at least 5 to 10 minutes more before removing lid.

3. To re-heat rice: Rice re-heats beautifully in a microwave, but if that is not available, then follow this procedure:

   In a large pan bring plenty of water to boil. Add the cold rice, stir for a minute and then drain thoroughly through a sieve. Return the rice to the pan. Cover and leave it on low heat for 3-4 minutes.

KHEERE AUR MOOLI KA SALAAD
cucumber and radish salad

YOU WILL NEED

$^1/_2$ cucumber

6-8 small red radishes

1 tsp lemon juice

pinch freshly milled pepper

$^1/_8$ tsp salt, or to taste

A combination of two or three raw vegetables makes a simple accompaniment to any cooked meal.

Wash the cucumber but leave the skin on. Cut it into wedges.

Wash the radishes and cut them into halves. Arrange in a serving bowl or platter, sprinkle with lemon juice, salt and pepper. Chill slightly and serve.

Handy Hint

Red chilli powder may be substituted for black pepper and rock salt for ordinary salt.

MAZEDAR KELE
banana surprise

YOU WILL NEED

8 bananas

8 tbsp butter

4 tbsp soft brown sugar

1/2 tsp grated nutmeg

a pinch of ground cinnamon

juice of 4 oranges

cream (optional)

This baked banana recipe will never cease to delight. In spite of the combination of different flavours the result is marvellous.

Peel the bananas and cut them in half lengthwise. Heat butter in a large frying pan (non-stick if possible) and fry the bananas gently for a minute or two. Remove and transfer to a shallow oven-proof dish.

Mix the orange juice with the brown sugar, cinnamon and nutmeg. Pour this mixture over the bananas and bake uncovered in a very hot oven for 15-20 minutes or until the juice thickens and coats the bananas.

Serve with cream if desired—but the bananas are nice to eat just with an extra spoonful of the hot thick syrup around them.

Handy Hint
The bananas are excellent if served with a little thick custard or some ice-cream for a change.

Formal Lunch For Vegetarians

RAJMAH *Red Kidney Beans*	**KAIRI KI CHUTNEY** *Green Mango Chutney*
TOORAI KA SAALAN *Steamed Courgettes*	**PAAPADS** *Poppadums*
PALAK PANEER *Indian Cottage Cheese and Spinach Curry*	**BADAAM KI BARFI** *Almond Fudge*
PEELE ZEERE WALE CHAWAL *Yellow Savoury Rice*	**NAMKEEN LASSI** *Savoury Buttermilk*

Serves four to six people

RAJMAH
red kidney beans

Kidney beans are eaten virtually all over the globe. They are inexpensive and provide high food value besides having a superb taste and attractive colouring.

YOU WILL NEED

1 lb (450 g) red kidney beans (the deeper the colour the better)

3 pints (1.8 litres) water for boiling

$\frac{1}{2}$ tsp turmeric powder

$\frac{1}{2}$ tsp chilli powder

1 tbsp salt

FOR THE GRAVY

3 oz (75 g) ghee (preferably) or cooking oil

3 green cardamoms

4 cloves

4 oz (115 g) onions, peeled and grated

2 oz (50 g) ginger, peeled and grated

2 cloves garlic, finely minced

4 oz (115 g) canned tomatoes chopped or 2 tbsp tomato puree

To cook the beans
Wash and soak beans for at least 6-8 hours, preferably overnight, before cooking.

To pressure cook: Put all ingredients together in a pressure cooker and cook at 15 lbs pressure for approximately 25 minutes, or till beans are tender.

To cook in a pan: Use a large pan, and boil beans rapidly for 10 minutes then reduce heat to low cover and simmer for 30-40 minutes until beans are tender. (Add a little more hot water if required.)

It is very important to ensure that kidney beans are thoroughly cooked before they are eaten.

For the gravy
Heat ghee in a saucepan, add cardamoms and cloves. When they swell a little add grated onions and fry until they begin to turn pinkish; add ginger and garlic and fry until golden brown, stirring frequently.

Add tomatoes/tomato puree and fry further for a few minutes, until ghee separates from the mixture.

Add the cooked beans along with their cooking liquid and if the gravy seems insufficient add a little more boiling water. Cover and cook on low heat for a further 5-10 minutes. Sprinkle garam masala and coriander leaves and always serve rajmah hot.

Contd. ....

1 tbsp garam masala powder

GARNISH

Few green coriander leaves

Handy Hints

1. Rajmah freezes exceedingly well. It can be easily defrosted and reheated without any loss of taste or flavour.

2. Why not try "rajmah on toast" instead of "beans on toast" next time? We assure you it will make a wonderful change.

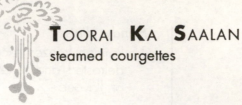

TOORAI KA SAALAN
steamed courgettes

YOU WILL NEED

1 lb (450 g) medium sized courgettes, peeled and cut into $\frac{1}{4}$" thick (0.5 cm) rounds

3 oz (75 g) onions, peeled and sliced

4 oz (115 g) medium sized tomatoes, roughly chopped

$\frac{1}{2}$" (1.25 cm) fresh ginger, peeled and chopped

1-2 green chillies, chopped

1 tbsp butter

1 tsp salt, or to taste

$\frac{1}{2}$ tsp turmeric powder

1 tbsp green coriander leaves, chopped

This particular dish tastes much better when made in a pressure cooker and needs only 2-3 minutes to cook.

Put all ingredients in a pressure cooker. Mix and cook for two minutes at 15 lbs pressure. Turn off the heat and let the pressure drop by itself.

If too much liquid remains, return to high heat, uncover and cook until it is semi-dry.

If not using a pressure cooker, use a pan with a tight-fitting lid instead. In this case, fry the onions in butter first and then add the rest of the ingredients, cover and cook on medium heat for approximately 8-10 minutes.

Handy Hints

1. Just before serving, add an extra knob of butter to give this dish a nice sheen.

2. To vary the flavour slightly, sprinkle $\frac{1}{4}$ tsp (1.25 ml) dry roasted cumin seeds over the finished dish.

Makhani Murgh

Rajmah, Urad Ki Dal

Chane Aur Lauki Ki Dal

Mushrooms

Tamatar, Lahsun Chutney

The Complete Indian Menu

Drinks

PALAK PANEER
indian cottage cheese and spinach curry

Many of the best-loved vegetarian dishes are made by combining vegetables with paneer (home-made Indian cottage cheese.) The combination of spinach and paneer is a highly successful one—the dish looks good and tastes even better!

YOU WILL NEED

1 ¹/₂ lbs (875 g) fresh or 1 lb (450 g) chopped frozen spinach

6 oz (175 g) paneer/tofu (see page 7 and 8)

4 tbsp vegetable cooking oil

6 fl oz (180 ml) boiling water

3 oz (90 g) onions, peeled and finely sliced

³/₄ oz (20 g) ginger, scraped and shredded

1-2 cloves garlic, crushed, (optional)

1-2 green chillies (or more if wanted), finely chopped

4 oz (120 g) tomatoes, skinned and chopped

1 tsp salt, or to taste

¹/₄ tsp chilli powder

¹/₄ tsp turmeric powder

6 fl oz (180 ml) milk

1 tbsp double cream

If using fresh spinach, wash leaves very thoroughly, steam and puree. Keep aside. If using frozen spinach, defrost, puree and keep aside.

Heat oil in a saucepan and fry onions until lightly browned. Add the ginger, garlic and green chillies and fry for a minute or two, but do not let them brown.

Stir in the tomatoes and fry until they soften. Add salt, turmeric and chilli powders and stir and fry till oil begins to separate. Add the pureed spinach and mix well with the fried masala. Pour in the milk and water and mix thoroughly. Simmer on low heat for about 7-8 minutes.

Stir in the paneer/tofu pieces. Cover and cook for a further 3-4 minutes.

Remove from heat, and transfer to a serving dish. Just before serving pour the cream on top giving it a gentle swirl.

Handy Hints

1. For an even richer taste, the pieces of paneer are usually shallow fried to a golden brown, before they are added to the spinach.

2. Instead of paneer, a handful of large dry roasted and split peanuts may be used and the resulting dish will no longer be palak paneer but moongphalli paneer.

Peele Zeere Wale Chawal
yellow savoury rice

You Will Need

9 oz (250 g) Basmati rice or any good quality long grain rice

18 fl oz (540 ml) water

1 tbsp ghee, or vegetable cooking oil

1 tsp black cumin seeds

$\frac{1}{2}$ tsp turmeric powder

$\frac{1}{2}$ tsp salt

Adding a touch of colour to any rice dish makes it look more interesting. As yellow is considered to be auspicious by most Indians, it is the favourite colour choice. Saffron is reserved for special occasions, as it is rather expensive. For everyday use, turmeric is a satisfactory natural alternative for imparting colour to any dish.

Clean and wash the rice in several changes of water, rubbing the rice gently between the fingers until the water runs clear.

Drain and soak rice in the measured amount of water and leave it to stand for 15-20 minutes. Drain the rice through a sieve and save the water for later use.

Now heat ghee/oil in a large saucepan, add the cumin seeds and when they splutter, remove pan from heat. Add the turmeric and immediately afterwards add the drained rice. Stir and fry gently for 2-3 minutes till all the grains are well coated with oil. Add salt and the reserved water.

Bring the rice to boil. Stir gently once. Cover with a tight-fitting lid, reduce heat to very low, and cook for 10-12 minutes. Remove from heat. Leave covered and undisturbed for a further 5 minutes. Serve hot.

Handy Hint

The turmeric may be omitted altogether if desired—without affecting the flavour of this dish. In this case you will simply have cumin flavoured (white) rice.

KAIRI KI CHUTNEY
green mango chutney

YOU WILL NEED

4 oz (115 g) raw green mango, peeled and sliced

2 oz (55 g) fresh green coriander leaves

2 green chillies

1 desp sugar

1 tsp salt

1 tbsp onion, peeled and chopped

1-2 tbsp water

Some form of chutney is a necessary accompaniment to every Indian meal. Being piquant in taste it stimulates the appetite and is believed to promote digestion. Most chutneys are based on fresh herbs and are uncooked.

Mix all the ingredients together and liquidize. The chutney will keep in the fridge for 3-4 days.

Handy Hint
This chutney freezes well.

PAAPADS
poppadums

YOU WILL NEED

4-6 paapads (plain or spicy)

a hot grill and a pair of tongs

Paapads are light, crisp, savoury wafers which seem to have no counterpart in other cuisines. They are typically made from pulses such as urad (black beans) and moong (dried green beans), but others made from rice, sago, potatoes etc., are not uncommon. In fact, every region has its own special type of paapad and the variety is quite enormous.

As making paapad from scratch is a highly skilled and labour intensive process, most people prefer to buy readymade paapads, which can then be cooked within seconds.

Turn on the grill to its highest setting. Place paapad on the grill tray as close to the source of heat as possible. Within seconds, it will increase in size and light brown specks will appear on the surface. Using tongs, turn it over for a further 3-5 seconds. Remove and serve immediately.

Paapads need careful watching over as they burn easily.

Handy Hints
1. To microwave: Place paapad on a plate. Turn on full power for 30 seconds.

2. To deep fry: Immerse paapad in plenty of hot oil for a few seconds. Remove and drain on absorbent kitchen paper before serving.

3. Paapads tend to lose their crispness and go soft if the atmosphere is damp—so it is best to cook them just before serving; otherwise cool and store in an airtight tin.

BADAAM KI BARFI
almond fudge

YOU WILL NEED

³/₄ pint (425 ml) full cream milk

4 oz (115 g) ground almond powder

4 oz (115 g) sugar

2 oz (60 g) full cream milk powder

2 green cardamoms, peeled and crushed

2 dozen blanched almonds

Barfi is one of the most popular and commonly made sweetmeats of India. Perhaps the nearest equivalent to barfi is fudge, in that they are both milk-based and require fair amounts of sugar. Like most other Indian sweetmeats, barfi can be served as a dessert or as a tea time snack.

In a heavy-based pan, boil the milk. Add the ground almond powder and boil quickly till mixture thickens (approximately 15-20 minutes.) Stir frequently to prevent it from sticking.

Add the milk powder, sugar, and cardamoms and stirring continuously cook for a further 5-6 minutes, or till the mixture is fairly stiff (almost like a soft dough) and begins to leave the sides of the pan.

Spread mixture on a pre-greased dish with slightly raised edges, and decorate with blanched and slivered almonds.

When cool and set, cut into diamond shapes. Store in an air-tight container. It will keep in the fridge for a week or so.

Handy Hint
To vary, use chopped pistachio nuts instead of slivered almonds.

NAMKEEN LASSI
savoury buttermilk

YOU WILL NEED

5 fl oz (180 ml) natural yoghurt

$^1/_4$ tsp salt, or to taste

pinch freshly milled black pepper

$1^1/_4$ pints (750 ml) cold water

10 oz (275 g) ice cubes

Lassi is an age-old beverage of India which has stood the test of time, and has only recently been introduced as a healthy yoghurt drink to the West. It is cooling and light, and may be served with a meal or on its own at any time as a thirst quencher.

Whisk together the yoghurt, salt and pepper. Add cold water and whisk again. Check seasoning—it should have the merest hint of a savoury taste. Pour the lassi in a jug and serve chilled with ice cubes.

Handy Hints

1. If serving lassi on its own i.e., (not with a meal), a pinch of rock salt and a garnish of 3-4 mint leaves will give it a delightful flavour.

2. To vary the flavour, add a large pinch of dry roasted and powdered cumin seeds and 4-5 finely chopped mint leaves to the basic recipe given above. It makes a very refreshing drink.

Formal Lunch For Non-Vegetarians

MAKHANI MURGH *Cream Chicken*	**PAAPAD** *Poppadums* *(For details see page 38)*
SHAAMI KABAB *Minced Meat* *Cutlets*	**HARE DHANIA KI** **CHUTNEY** *Green Coriander* *Chutney*
DHULI URAD KI DAAL *Split Black Bean* *Curry*	**SHRIKHAND** *Creamed Yoghurt* *Dessert*
NAAN *Leavened Baked* *Bread*	**NIMBU PAANI** *Fresh Lime Drink*

Serves four to six people

MAKHANI MURGH
cream chicken

Cream chicken is made on special occasions only as it is an exceedingly delectable dish which tends to be a little on the expensive side. It is a popular item on the menus of many leading Indian restaurants.

YOU WILL NEED

1 1/2 lb (700 g) chicken pieces, (preferably breast)

8 oz (225 g) double cream

6 oz (175 g) canned tomatoes

2 oz (50 g) fresh root ginger

4 cloves garlic

2 tbsp   natural yoghurt

1/2 tsp turmeric powder

1 tsp roasted ground coriander seeds

2 tbsp mix dried fruits such as raisins, currants and sultanas (optional)

1 tbsp butter

pinch red colouring

1 tsp salt, or to taste

1/4 tsp red chilli powder

2 sheets beaten silver leaves (optional)

Special Requirements

A large, heavy-based pan, liquidizer and a wooden spatula.

Remove skin, wash and dry the chicken pieces and place them in the pan.

Put all the remaining ingredients except the coriander seeds, dry fruit and butter in a liquidizer and switch it on for a minute or two.

Pour the above mixture over the chicken pieces and set the pan on high heat for about 5 minutes. Stir gently with the wooden spatula, taking care not to break the chicken pieces.

As the chicken needs to be cooked without the addition of any further liquid, cover the pan with a tight-fitting lid, reduce heat and cook until the chicken is tender and nearly all the liquid has dried off. (Dried fruits to be added if using.) Then add the butter and fry for another 2 or 3 minutes.

Sprinkle the coriander powder just before serving and decorate with the silver leaves.

Handy Hints

1. To vary, add 8 oz (225 g) of frozen, finely chopped spinach, if available. Defrost spinach and pile it over the liquidized tomato/yoghurt/ cream mixture and then proceed as above.
2. By adding spinach, one can easily increase the number of helpings in order to accommodate any last minute guests.

SHAAMI KABAB
minced meat cutlets

These classic mince cutlets are a perfect cocktail choice, but may equally well be served as part of a main meal.

You Will Need

1 lb (450 g) minced lamb

3 oz (90 g) onions, peeled and chopped

1" (2.5 cm) fresh root ginger, sliced

3 cloves garlic, peeled and chopped

2 bay leaves

$^1/_2$ tsp chilli powder

2 tbsp yellow split peas/ Bengal gram

2-3 green chillies

2 cloves

1" cinnamon

2 whole brown cardamoms

1 tsp salt, or to taste

1 tbsp lemon juice

12 fl oz (360 ml) water

vegetable cooking oil for shallow frying

Special Requirements
Heavy-based saucepan, griddle and food processor

Place all the ingredients except oil and lemon juice in a heavy-based saucepan, cover and cook on medium heat for 10 minutes. Then reduce heat, and continue cooking for a further 15 minutes or so until all the liquid has dried up and the mince is cooked. (If not cooked, add a little more water, cover and cook until dry.) Stir the mixture occasionally to prevent it from sticking to the bottom of the pan. The mince mixture must be quite dry, or else the kababs will be difficult to handle and will break up easily.

Remove the cinnamon, bay leaves and the shells of the cardamoms. Add lemon juice, and check and adjust seasoning if required.

Grind the cooked mince by pounding or processing it in a food processor until a dough-like mixture is formed. Divide it into 12 portions, shape each into a round ball and then flatten it between the palms.

Set the griddle on medium heat, and lightly grease its base with 1 tbsp oil. Shallow fry the kababs in two batches. Dribble a little oil around the edges of the kababs until they are golden brown in colour. Turn the kababs over and repeat the process.

Serve hot with a green chutney.

Contd. ....

Handy Hints

1. To cut down on cooking time the mince may be initially cooked in a pressure cooker for 10 minutes, then cooked uncovered until any remaining liquid dries off. The rest of the procedure remains the same.

2. Shammi kababs freeze extremely well so it is worth making a large batch at a time. They may be re-heated straightaway in the microwave or in a hot oven for a few minutes.

3. If desired the centre of each of the kababs may be filled with a little of the following mixture: $1^1/_2$ tbsp finely chopped fresh coriander leaves, $^1/_4$" peeled and grated ginger, 1 tbsp very finely minced onion, 1-2 finely minced green chillies and a large pinch of salt.

The result is well worth the extra trouble.

Dhuli Hui Urad Ki Daal
split black bean curry

This daal when cooked, has a deliciously smooth and delicate texture. It is high in proteins and vitamins especially vitamins A and B.

You Will Need

8 oz (225 g) split black beans without skin

1 pint (600 ml) water

1 ½ tsp turmeric powder

½ tsp red chilli powder

1 tsp salt, or to taste

1 tbsp lemon juice

1 oz (30 g) ghee

4 oz (115 g) onions, peeled and sliced into fine rings

pinch asafoetida

1 tbsp chopped green coriander leaves

1 green chilli, finely chopped

1 oz (25 g) ginger, scraped and cut into very fine slivers

Remove any grit from the black beans and wash them two or three times in fresh changes of water.

Put the daal in a heavy saucepan along with the water, turmeric and chilli powders. Cover and allow the beans to cook. If necessary, add a little more water so that the beans tenderize and all the liquid is absorbed.

Add salt and lemon juice. Mix well. Turn out into a serving dish.

Heat ghee in a frying pan and when hot fry the onion rings until crisp and browned. Remove the onion rings and keep them aside. Re-heat the same ghee, add a pinch of asafoetida and stir for a few seconds. Then pour the hot ghee over the cooked daal. Mix thoroughly and cover for 3-4 minutes.

Serve the daal hot, garnished with fried onion rings, finely chopped green coriander leaves, green chillies, and slivered ginger.

NAAN
leavened baked bread

YOU WILL NEED

1 lb (450 g) plain flour

1 tsp baking powder

1/4 oz (6 g) dried yeast or
1/2 oz (15 g) fresh yeast

pinch salt

1 tsp sugar

2 fl oz (55 ml) milk

2 fl oz (55 ml) melted ghee

2 eggs, lightly beaten

2 fl oz (55 ml) natural yoghurt

1/2 tsp nigella seeds

Naans were introduced to the Indian scene centuries ago by the Muslim invaders from the Middle East, but have now become an integral part of Indian cuisine. They are rich, leavened breads, almost always teardrop shaped and traditionally baked in a clay oven. For the sake of convenience, an electric or a gas oven may also be used.

Sift together the flour, baking powder, yeast, salt and sugar in a bowl.

Warm the milk in a saucepan. Remove from heat and add ghee, lightly beaten eggs and yoghurt. Mix thoroughly.

With the help of this mixture (using only as much as is necessary) make a soft, pliable dough. Knead very thoroughly for at least 5 minutes until the dough is smooth and elastic. Form into a ball, brush with a little melted ghee, cover with a damp cloth and leave in a warm place for at least 3 to 4 hours to double in size.

Pre-heat oven to 230° C (Gas mark 8). Knead the dough once again (lightly) and divide it into 8 equal parts. Dust your hands with a little flour and shape each portion into a round.

Take one ball at a time, flatten and roll it into a tear drop shape, approximately 9" (23 cm) long and 5" (13 cm) wide. Brush upper surface lightly with water and sprinkle a few nigella seeds over it, pressing them in lightly.

Place 2 (or if space permits, 3) rolled out naans on a baking tray leaving a little space between them. Put them in the pre-heated oven for approximately

Contd. ....

5 minutes or until golden spots appear on the surface.

Remove and serve immediately for the best results. However, they can also be baked in batches, wrapped in foil and re-heated in a hot oven just before serving.

Handy Hint

Alternatively, the naans may also be cooked under a grill. Pre-heat grill, to its highest setting, and have ready a hot heavy-based griddle, whilst rolling out the naans.

Lightly brush one side of a rolled out naan with water and place the moistened surface on the hot griddle. Brush the top with a little melted ghee and sprinkle some of the nigella seeds over it. When the underside is cooked and golden brown in colour, transfer the naan to the hot grill with the help of a spatula, keeping the nigella side as close as possible to the grill. When the surface acquires brown spots, remove and serve immediately or stack in a clean tea towel to keep them warm.

Hare Dhania Ki Chutney
green coriander chutney

You Will Need

4 oz (115 g) fresh green leaves, washed

3-4 green chillies, or less for a milder chutney

1 tsp salt

1 tsp sugar

1 tbsp lemon juice, preferably freshly squeezed

2 tbsp water

This refreshing chutney is ideal for those who appreciate the distinctive fragrance of green coriander leaves. What is better, it can be prepared in next to no time.

Mix all the ingredients together and liquidize. The chutney will keep well for 3-4 days in the fridge.

SHRIKHAND
creamed yoghurt dessert

YOU WILL NEED

1 pint (600 ml) wholemilk natural yoghurt

4-6 oz (100-175 g) castor sugar, or to taste

1 tsp saffron soaked in 1 tbsp warm milk

2-3 green cardamoms, shelled and seeds powdered

2 tbsp almonds, blanched and shredded

2 tbsp pistachios

This delightful creamy dessert from Maharashtra in Western India is based on strained yoghurt, while saffron gives it that exquisite flavour and colour.

Special requirement
Piece of muslin 20"x 20" (50 cm x 50 cm) approximately

Place the yoghurt in the muslin square. Draw up the corners and tie a knot. Suspend the muslin bag (e.g. over a kitchen sink) for 4-6 hours or overnight and allow the liquid to drain away.

Place this thick yoghurt in a large bowl and add the sugar gradually, beating it in thoroughly until all the sugar has dissolved and a soft creamy consistency is achieved. Check the sweetness and if required add a little more sugar and beat again.

Crush the saffron and mix it into the yoghurt along with the powdered cardamom seeds and half of the nuts.

Pour into individual serving dishes and top with the remaining nuts. Chill lightly before serving.

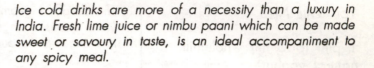

NIMBU PAANI
fresh lime drink

YOU WILL NEED

2 ¹/₂ fl oz (75 ml) juice of freshly squeezed lime or lemon

30 fl oz (900 ml) water

1 oz (30 g) castor sugar or 1 tsp salt, according to taste

pinch rock salt/black salt

ice cubes

TO GARNISH

lime or lemon slices

Ice cold drinks are more of a necessity than a luxury in India. Fresh lime juice or nimbu paani which can be made sweet or savoury in taste, is an ideal accompaniment to any spicy meal.

Mix lime or lemon juice, water, sugar/salt and rock salt thoroughly. Serve with ice cubes and a twist of lime or lemon slices.

Handy Hints

1. For that extra touch, add a few mint leaves as garnish.

2. A sprinkling of freshly ground black pepper can further add to the flavour, if you are making the savoury nimbu paani.

If you are making sweet nimbu paani it is much easier if you dissolve the sugar in water first. The addition of the lemon juice prevents it dissolving as quickly.

Simple Dinner for Vegetarians

DHULI MOONG KI DAAL
Split Green Gram

SOOKHI BHINDI
Sauted Okra

ALOO KA RAITA
Potatoes in Yoghurt

BAGHARE CHAWAL
Seasoned Rice

MILE JULE TAZE PHAL
Mixed Fresh Fruit

ILAICHI WALI CHAI
Cardamom Flavoured Tea

Serves four to six people.

DHULI MOONG KI DAAL
split green gram

This daal is a great favourite because of its delicate taste and flavour. Being easily digestible, it is highly recommended for invalids and babies.

YOU WILL NEED

8 oz (225 g) split green gram

1 1/4 pint (750 ml) water

1/2 tsp turmeric powder

1/2 tsp chilli powder

1 tsp salt, or to taste

1 oz (30 g) butter or ghee

1 oz (30 g) onions, peeled and finely chopped

2 oz (60 g) tomatoes, skinned and chopped

1 tbsp fresh coriander leaves, finely chopped

Clean and wash daal. Put it in a saucepan along with water, turmeric and chilli powders. Bring to boil and cook till daal is soft and reduced to a creamy consistency. (This takes approximately 15 minutes.) Remove from heat, add salt and keep aside.

In a frying pan melt butter/ghee and fry onions till golden brown. Add the chopped tomatoes and fry further for a few minutes till the tomatoes are soft and mushy. Pour this mixture over the cooked daal and mix gently.

Serve hot, garnished with coriander leaves.

SOOKHI BHINDI
sauted okra

YOU WILL NEED

1 lb (450 g) okra/bhindi

3 tbsp vegetable cooking oil

2 oz (60g) onions, peeled and sliced

1/2 tsp salt

1/4 chilli powder

1/2 tsp dried mango powder

Bhindi or okra has acquired an exotic image in the West, but is in fact one of the most commonly grown vegetables in India, relished by both vegetarians and non-vegetarians alike.

Whenever using okra, wash and dry them thoroughly before chopping, as any moisture present will produce an excessive amount of sticky sap. Top and tail okra and cut them into 1/4" (0.5 cm) rounds.

Heat vegetable oil in a frying pan or kadhai and saute the onions. Stir in the okra, chilli powder and salt. Stir and fry over high heat till moisture from the sap has nearly dried off.

Reduce heat, cover and cook for a further 3-4 minutes or till the okra is tender—but not mushy. Do not add any water. Sprinkle mango powder over it , mix gently and serve hot.

Handy Hint
To vary the above recipe add a few very finely diced potatoes, and a pinch of turmeric powder to the fried onions; then add the okra.

ALOO KA RAITA
potatoes in yoghurt

YOU WILL NEED

6 oz (175 g) potatoes

pinch red chilli powder, or
to taste

10 fl oz (300 ml) natural
yoghurt (unsweetened)

1 tsp salt, or to taste

$^1/_4$ tsp freshly milled black
pepper

$^1/_4$ tsp cumin seeds

The use of natural yoghurt has always been a part of Indian cuisine since time immemorial. Indians firmly believe that yoghurt is good for health and therefore consume it extensively in various forms. In fact, no meal seems to be complete without yoghurt.

Raitas are side dishes and are made by the addition of suitable raw or cooked ingredients to natural yoghurt. They have a soothing and cooling effect and provide a marked contrast to the rest of the spicy food.

Boil, peel and dice potatoes into $^1/_2$" (1.25 cm) cubes. Allow to cool.

In a frying pan, dry roast cumin seeds (without adding any oil) till they start to splutter and darken a little. Remove and grind to a powder.

Whisk the yoghurt with salt till smooth and creamy. Add diced potatoes and cumin seed powder and mix gently.

Garnish with chilli powder and freshly milled black pepper sprinkled over the yoghurt mixture. Chill and serve.

Handy Hint
If preparing this dish in advance, it is best to add salt at the last moment as this prevents the yoghurt from becoming sour.

BAGHARE CHAWAL
seasoned rice

YOU WILL NEED

9 oz (250 g) Basmati rice

18 fl oz (540 ml) water

2 tbsp ghee or vegetable cooking oil

4-5 cloves

3-4 green cardamoms

1" piece (2.5 cm) cinnamon

2-3 bay leaves

6-8 peppercorns

1 tsp salt

The use of whole spices for seasoning makes this dish very aromatic and inviting.

Clean and wash rice in several changes of water, running your fingers through the rice till the water runs clear.

Drain and soak rice in the measured amount of water and leave it to stand for 15-20 minutes. Then drain the rice through a sieve and reserve the water for later use.

In a large heavy-based pan, heat ghee or oil and add the whole spices and bay leaves. Stir and fry for a few seconds till they begin to splutter. Add drained rice and salt and fry gently for 2-3 minutes till all the grains are well coated with ghee/oil. Add the reserved water, turn heat up to high and bring to a boil.

Stir the rice gently once, cover with a tight-fitting lid, reduce heat to low and cook for 10 to 12 minutes. Remove pan from heat and leave undisturbed for a further 5 minutes. Serve hot.

Handy Hints
1. If Basmati rice is not available, use any available long grain rice. The spices will still lift and enhance the flavour of the lesser quality rice.

2. To re-heat rice, cover and place in a pre-heated medium oven for approximately 8 minutes or in a microwave for 2-3 minutes on full power.

MILE JULE TAZE PHAL
mixed fresh fruit

YOU WILL NEED

A combination of any of 3 or 4 of the following:

mango skinned, stoned and sliced

papaya skinned, de-seeded and sliced or cubed

guava cubed or cut into wedges

lychees peeled and stoned

pineapple sliced or cubed

grapes halved and deseeded

pomegranate outer skin and inner papery membranes removed

apple cored and sliced

peaches stoned and quartered

pears cored and sliced

plums stoned and halved

oranges peeled and cut into segments

A mixture of fresh fruit provides a cool and refreshing end to an informal lunch. Any of the typically Indian fruits may be used.

Prepare fruit. Mix gently, chill and serve.

ILAICHI WALI CHAI
cardamom flavoured tea

YOU WILL NEED

2-3 green cardamoms

1 tsp sugar (optional)

2-3 tea bags or 6 tsp Darjeeling tea leaves

pot of boiling water

milk and sugar (as required)

Any time is tea time! And tea may be served in a variety of flavours with cardamom topping the list.

Always warm the teapot first by pouring in some boiling water, then drain it away.

Into the warmed up teapot put the green cardamoms, sugar (if using) and tea bags/tea leaves. Pour in boiling water. Cover the teapot and let it stand for 3-4 minutes for the flavours to develop.

Strain and serve tea as required with or without milk and sugar.

Simple Dinner for Non-Vegetarians

BHUNA KHEEMA
Dry Mince Curry

TAMATAR ALOO KI TARKARI
Tomato and Potato Curry

KHEERE AUR PYAZ KA RAITA
Cucumber and Onion Yoghurt

SADA PARATHA
Shallow Fried Unleavened Bread

DAHI AUR KELA
Banana Yoghurt

ESPRESSO STYLE COFFEE
Indian Style Espresso

Serves four to six people

Bhuna Kheema
dry mince curry

You Will Need

1 ¹/₂ oz (45 g) vegetable cooking oil

1 lb (450 g) lean minced lamb

3-4 cloves

3 green cardamoms

¹/₂ tsp black cumin seeds

3 oz (90 g) onions, peeled and finely sliced

1 tsp salt, or to taste

¹/₄ tsp turmeric powder

1-2 fat cloves of garlic, very finely minced or crushed

2 green chillies, finely chopped

1/2 oz (15 g) fresh root ginger, finely grated

1/2 tsp chilli powder

5 fl oz (150 ml) hot water

1 desp fresh lime juice

1 tbsp fresh green coriander leaves, finely chopped

Bhuna kheema is an easy to prepare and homely dish that goes well with parathas.

Heat the vegetable oil in a heavy-based pan. Add the cloves, cardamoms and cumin seeds. Fry for a few seconds then add the chopped onions. Stir and fry until the onions are light brown then add the ginger, garlic and green chillies. Continue frying for 1-2 minutes. Next add turmeric and chilli powders, and salt, followed by the minced lamb after a few seconds. Stir and fry until mince is browned and all the liquid released by it has dried up.

Add hot water, cover and continue cooking on slow heat until lamb is done and the water is all absorbed.

Remove from heat, add lemon juice and chopped coriander leaves. Mix well and serve hot.

Handy Hint
Alternatively, use a pressure cooker to save time.

Put all ingredients except water, lemon juice and coriander leaves in the pressure cooker, close lid and bring to 15 lbs pressure and cook for 10 minutes. Allow pressure to drop by itself; open lid and return cooker to heat. All the juices will have dried up by this time. Fry (without adding any more oil) until the mixture is well browned. Add hot water, and simmer for 2-3 minutes. Add lemon juice and coriander leaves and serve.

TAMATAR ALOO KI TARKARI
tomato and potato curry

Indian cooking is known for its flexibility. Any basic recipe can be altered ever so slightly to present a whole new look. In this recipe, the onions, which are usually grated and fried with the spices have been substituted with whole button onions.

YOU WILL NEED

8 oz (225 g) new potatoes, (marble sized ones)

4 oz (115 g) button onions

4-6 fl oz (115 -170 ml) vegetable cooking oil

$^1/_2$ tsp cumin seeds

$^1/_2$ tsp mustard seeds

5-6 curry leaves

2 cloves garlic, finely chopped

$^1/_2$ tsp turmeric powder

$^1/_2$ tsp chilli powder

1 tsp salt, or to taste

1 tsp sugar

1 lb (450 g) tomatoes, chopped

2-3 green chillies, deseeded and sliced lengthwise

6 fl oz (180 ml) hot water

2 tbsp spring onions, stalks only, chopped

Wash and dry the potatoes and peel the button onions. Heat oil in a saucepan and fry the potatoes until golden brown. Remove and keep aside. In the same oil, fry the button onions until they turn pink. Remove and keep aside.

Reheat cooking oil. Add cumin and mustard seeds, followed after a few seconds, by the curry leaves and garlic. Stir and fry for a minute or so until the seeds begin to splutter. Reduce heat, add turmeric and chilli powders salt and sugar. Stir and fry, and a few seconds later, add the tomatoes. Increase heat and continue stirring and frying until the tomatoes begin to disintegrate.

Now add the green chillies and hot water. Cover and cook on low heat until all the ingredients are well blended and take on a slightly glossy appearance. Add the fried potatoes and button onions. Cover and cook on very low heat until the potatoes are done. Before serving, sprinkle with the chopped spring onion stalks.

Handy Hint
If new potatoes are not available, use any other variety cut into 1" (2.5 cm) cubes.

KHEERE AUR PYAZ KA RAITA
cucumber and onion yoghurt

✿ YOU WILL NEED

10 fl oz (285 ml) natural yoghurt

$^3/_4$ tsp salt, or to taste

$^1/_4$ tsp chilli powder

4 oz (115 g) coarsely grated cucumber, with skin

2 finely chopped spring onions along with their stalks

The combination of yoghurt and onions is most refreshing and an added bonus is that it hardly takes any time to prepare.

Whisk the yoghurt with salt and chilli powder until the yoghurt is smooth and creamy. Add the cucumber and spring onions. Chill and serve.

Handy Hint
Use a teaspoonful of finely minced onions if spring onions are not available.

SADA PARATHA
shallow fried wholemeal bread

You Will Need

14 oz (400 g) wholewheat flour

pinch salt

approx 20 fl oz (600 ml) water

4-6 fl oz (120-180 ml) ghee

2 oz (50 g) wholewheat flour for dusting and rolling out

A paratha is a shallow fried, wholemeal bread which may be served for breakfast, lunch or dinner. It is not for weight watchers, however, as a fair amount of ghee is required to make it crisp.

Sift 14 oz (400 g) flour and salt in a large bowl. Add sufficient water to form a soft, (but not sticky) dough. Knead well for 5 minutes. Cover and leave it to stand for half an hour.

Divide the dough into 12-14 equal parts and shape them into round balls. With the help of the remaining dry flour roll out each ball into a flat pancake about 5" (12 cm) in diameter. Coat the upper surface with a little melted ghee and fold it half into a semi-circle. Spread a little more ghee over the top surface and fold it twice again lengthwise. Press it down lightly, stretch it a little and make it into a cone-shaped spiral, keeping the folds on the outer side.

Press it down again in order to flatten it and roll it out, dusting as necessary with dry flour, into a paratha of 5-6" (12-15 cm) diameter.

Heat a griddle set on medium heat. Transfer paratha to hot griddle, and when the under surface is cooked, turn paratha over. Spread a little ghee on top and after a minute or so turn it over once again.

Now smear a little more ghee on top and cook on lowered heat until both sides are nicely browned and crisp.

Proceed to make the remaining parathas in the same way. Serve immediately to savour them at their best, as parathas lose their crispness if stored, though they

Contd. ....

still taste quite good even when they are cold.

Handy Hints

1. Parathas may be cooked in advance and stored in the fridge for two to three days. To re-heat and refresh them, return them to a hot griddle and shallow fry once again with less than a teaspoon or so of ghee in order to revive their crispness.

2. They may also be deep frozen, interleaved with grease-proof paper and overwrapped in aluminium foil, and re-heated in a microwave or hot oven for a few minutes.

3. Vegetable cooking oil may be used instead of ghee, if desired, but then the characteristic flavour of ghee will be missing.

DAHI AUR KELA
banana yoghurt

YOU WILL NEED

10 fl oz (285 ml) thick set
natural yoghurt

2-3 bananas

2 tbsp castor sugar

2-3 drops vanilla essence

No meal, however simple, is considered complete without something sweet at the end. Dahi aur kela is a quick and healthy dessert. Yoghurt based desserts have been popular in India since a very long time, and it is good to see that they are gaining popularity in the Western world as well!

Whisk the yoghurt until it is creamy. Add the castor sugar and vanilla essence and mix thoroughly.

Peel and slice bananas into $1/4$" (0.5 cm) rounds. Add these to the prepared yoghurt. Cover bowl with cling film, chill lightly and serve.

Handy Hint

If desired, a heaped tablespoonful of slivered, unsalted pistachio nuts or chopped cashewnuts or blanched and slivered almonds may be added.

ESPRESSO STYLE COFFEE
indian style espresso

YOU WILL NEED

4 heaped tsp instant coffee, (dark roasted)

4 tsp sugar, or more if required

1 tsp cold water

10 fl oz (300 ml) water

10 fl oz (300 ml) full cream milk

Coffee is grown extensively in the hilly regions of Southern India, and it is here that it is largely consumed. The following is a simple way of making espresso style coffee without the necessary gadgets.

In a small bowl mix the coffee, sugar and 1 tsp water. Beat vigorously with a teaspoon until the mixture is pale and slightly frothy. Add a few more drops of water if required.

In a milk pan, boil the milk and water together. Divide the coffee mixture into 4 cups and pour the boiling milk and water over the coffee from a height distance of four to six inches (10-18 cm). Stir gently and serve at once.

Handy Hint
Sprinkle a few grains of drinking chocolate on top for a slightly different effect.

Elaborate Dinner for Vegetarians

MILI JULI SABZION KI TIKKI
Mixed Vegetable Cutlets

MATAR PANEER
Home-Made Cheese and Peas Curry

DUM ALOO
Fried Potatoes in a Spicy Sauce

LAUKI AUR CHANE KI DAAL
Split Yellow Peas with White Gourd

MOONGPHALLI KI CHUTNEY
Peanut Chutney

HARA SALAAD
Green Salad

SHAHI PULAO
Saffron Flavoured Rice with Nuts

PURI
Deep Fried Wholemeal Bread

DOUBLE KA MITHA
Bread and Milk Pudding

JAL ZEERA
Appetizing Aromatic Drink

Serves six to eight people

MILI JULI SABZION KI TIKKI
mixed vegetable cutlets

You Will Need

2 large potatoes, boiled and roughly mashed

1 lb (450 g) mixed vegetables (peas, carrots, beans, cauliflower) chopped

2 tbsp onions or spring onions, finely chopped

1 tbsp fresh green coriander leaves, chopped

2 green chillies, deseeded and finely chopped, or $\frac{1}{2}$ tsp red chilli powder

1 tsp salt, or to taste

$\frac{1}{2}$ tsp garam masala powder

1 tsp lemon juice

2 $\frac{1}{2}$ oz (70 g) dried breadcrumbs

vegetable cooking oil for shallow frying

Cutlets are prepared from a host of ingredients which may be vegetarian or non-vegetarian. Because of the very large number of vegetarians in India, the many different types of vegetable tikki/cutlets come as no real surprise. The tikkis may be served both as snacks as well as side dishes to enhance a meal.

Steam the mixed vegetables in the minimum amount of water till tender. Drain fully and keep aside. Thoroughly mix the rest of the ingredients (except breadcrumbs and cooking oil) along with the vegetables and divide into 10 -12 equal portions.

Moisten palms of hand with a little water and flatten each portion of the vegetable mixture—either into a round or a pear shape as required. Roll in breadcrumbs and keep aside.

Heat a flat griddle or a heavy-based frying pan on medium heat. Shallow fry the cutlets till nicely browned on both sides.

Handy Hints

1. Frozen mixed vegetables can be used instead of fresh ones. Steam slightly before use.

2. Use the potato mixture as given for samosas on page 178 for making a different flavoured cutlet.

MATAR PANEER
home-made cheese and peas curry

YOU WILL NEED

8 oz (225 g) paneer/tofu

4 fl oz (115 ml) cooking oil

1 tsp cumin seeds

1/2 tsp coriander seeds

4 oz (115 g) onions/ peeled and grated

1 tsp salt, or to taste

1/2 tsp chilli powder

1 tbsp tomato puree (highly concentrated tomato pulp)

8 oz (225 g) shelled green peas

1 pint (600 ml) hot water

1 tbsp fresh green coriander leaves, finely chopped

Everybody loves matar paneer! The addition of this item to the menu turns a simple meal into a special one—more so for vegetarians. Matar paneer is often regarded as a most suitable alternative to any non-vegetarian dish.

Cut paneer into 1" (2.5 cm) cubes and deep fry in hot oil till golden brown. Drain and keep aside.

If using tofu instead of paneer, wash tofu in plenty of cold running water, dry thoroughly between sheets of paper towels and then cut into 1" (2.5 cm) cubes. Keep aside.

Heat oil and add cumin and coriander seeds, and when they begin to splutter, add the grated onions. Fry them till golden brown and stir in salt, red chilli powder and tomato puree. Stir and fry for a minute or so, and add a few tablespoons of hot water and fry further, stirring constantly, till a homogeneous mixture is obtained and oil begins to separate.

Add peas and fry for 2-3 minutes. Then add the remaining water, stir well, cover and cook for a few minutes, till peas are tender. Add the paneer/tofu. Cover and simmer gently for 3-4 minutes. Remove from heat.

Serve hot, garnished with chopped green coriander leaves.

Handy Hint
Instead of cutting paneer/tofu into cubes it may be crumbled and added to the masala—but in that case use only half the amount of water recommended. The end result should be dryish.

69

DUM ALOO
fried potatoes in a spicy sauce

Potato curry prepared by this method cannot be surpassed—both in taste and appearance. It is therefore an ideal dish to present at any festive occasion.

YOU WILL NEED

1 ¹/₂ lb (675 g) new potatoes (walnut-sized)

4 cloves garlic

1" piece (2.5 cm) fresh ginger

1 tbsp poppy seeds

1 tbsp almond powder

4 fl oz (115 ml) ghee

4 cloves

2 brown cardamoms

4 peppercorns

1" piece (2.5 cm) cinnamon

2-3 bay leaves

1 tsp coriander seeds

6 oz (170 g) onions, peeled and grated

¹/₂ tsp chilli powder

¹/₂ tsp turmeric powder

Wash and scrub potatoes, and dry them thoroughly. Prick them with a fork all over and deep fry in batches in hot vegetable cooking oil until golden brown. Remove and keep aside.

Grind ginger and garlic to a paste.

Dry roast poppy seeds on a hot griddle, till they start to splutter, but do not brown. Remove and grind them to a paste with the help of a little water. Add almond powder to this and keep aside.

In a large saucepan, heat ghee, and add cloves, cardamoms, cinnamon, peppercorns, crushed coriander seeds and bay leaves. Stir and fry for a few seconds until the cloves begin to swell. Add the grated onions and fry till golden brown. Add ginger and garlic paste and fry for a further minute. Sprinkle a tablespoon or two of hot water and stir continuously to prevent the mixture from sticking to the pan. Reduce heat, and add chilli powder, turmeric powder and salt. Stir and fry for a few seconds, adding another tablespoon or two of hot water, and return to medium heat.

Add the beaten yoghurt, 1 or 2 tablespoons at a time, and fry until all the yoghurt is absorbed, and ghee starts to separate. Add nutmeg, poppy seeds and almond powder. Fry for a few seconds and add potatoes. Mix gently and add the remaining hot water. Cover and cook on low heat till potatoes are

Contd. ....

1¹/₄ tsp salt, or to taste

4 oz (115 g) natural yoghurt, beaten

pinch nutmeg

10 fl oz (300 ml) water

vegetable cooking oil for deep frying

tender. Do not allow them to break up. If the sauce looks too dry, add a little more hot water as required.

Handy Hints

1. Dum aloo can be prepared a whole day in advance, if need be. In fact they taste better as all the flavours get infused to a greater extent.

2. The masala (i.e., the spice mixture) can be prepared and stored in an airtight container for 2-3 days in the fridge).

LAUKI AUR CHANE KI DAAL
split yellow peas and white gourd

Pulses are sometimes cooked with the addition of one or more vegetables. Such combinations, besides being wholesome, add interest and variety to a meal.

YOU WILL NEED

6 oz (170 g) Bengal gram

2 pints (1.2 litres) water

$1/_2$ tsp turmeric powder

$1/_2$ tsp chilli powder

$1/_2$ tsp coriander powder

1 tsp salt, or to taste

2 oz (55 g) white gourd, peeled and cut into 1" (2.5 cm) cubes

$1/_2$ tbsp lemon juice

2 tbsp cooking oil

1-2 whole red chillies

1 clove garlic, finely sliced

$1/_2$ tsp garam masala

Pick out any grit present in the gram and wash it thoroughly in water.

Put it along with water in a large pan: add turmeric, chilli and coriander powders, and bring to a boil. Cook until lentils are soft. Then add salt and white gourd, partially cover and cook further until the gourd is tender. Remove from heat, stir in the lemon juice and keep aside.

In a small frying pan, heat the oil and add the whole red chillies and sliced garlic. Fry for a few seconds till the garlic is light golden brown, immediately remove pan from heat, add the garam masala powder and pour the entire contents of the pan over the cooked daal. Cover daal at once and leave for a few minutes. Serve hot—the whole chillies are meant for seasoning only and should be removed before eating.

Handy Hint
Finely chopped spinach may be substituted for the white gourd.

MOONGPHALLI KI CHUTNEY
peanut chutney

You Will Need

2 oz (55 g) unsalted roasted peanuts

3-4 small whole red chillies

2-3 cloves garlic

$^1\!/_2$ tsp dry roasted cumin seeds

1 tbsp brown sugar or molasses

1 tsp salt, or to taste

1 tsp tamarind paste

2 tbsp water

Seasoning (Optional)

$^1\!/_4$ tsp mustard seeds

3-4 curry leaves

1 tsp vegetable oil

Moongphalli or peanut chutney is typically South Indian except that the proportion of red chillies used by the South Indians themselves would probably be three to four times as much as that recommended in this more moderate recipe.

Grind all the ingredients together coarsely. Check and adjust seasoning, adding a little more salt if necessary.

Optional seasoning
Heat oil in a small saucepan or in a large ladle. When hot, add mustard seeds and curry leaves, brown and pour over ground chutney.

Handy Hint
This chutney can be stored in the fridge for upto a week in an air-tight container.

HARA SALAAD
green salad

YOU WILL NEED

1 crisp lettuce

1 bunch spring onions

1 capsicum (green)

1 lime, sliced

FOR SEASONING

1 tbsp lemon juice

1/4 tsp salt

1 tsp coarsely ground mustard grains

Wash and prepare the salad ingredients as desired. Place in a serving bowl. Combine the ingredients for the seasoning and pour over the salad. Toss lightly and serve chilled.

SHAHI PULAO
saffron flavoured rice with nuts

This is a rice dish fit for an emperor hence the name shahi pulao. It is delicately flavoured with saffron, while the addition of whole nuts such as pistachios, almonds and cashewnuts gives it that extra touch of luxury.

You Will Need

9 oz (250 g) Basmati rice

18 fl oz (540 ml) water

1 oz (25 g) ghee

2 oz (55 g) whole blanched almonds

1 oz (25 g) cashewnuts, halved

1 oz (25 g) shelled, unsalted pistachios

4 green cardamoms

1 tsp salt

few strands saffron soaked in 1 tbsp water

2-3 silver leaves (optional)

Clean and wash the rice in several changes of water, rubbing the rice gently between the fingers, until the water runs clear.

Drain and soak the rice for 15-20 minutes in the measured amount of water. Drain rice once again over a sieve, but save this water for cooking.

Heat ghee in a heavy-based saucepan, and fry all the nuts until golden brown. Remove the nuts and keep aside.

To the same ghee in the pan, add green cardamoms and fry for a few seconds, then add the pre-soaked and drained rice. Stir gently and fry for a further 3-4 minutes until all the grains are well coated with ghee. Add salt, saffron and half of the fried nuts. Add the reserved water and bring the rice to boil, allowing it to cook on high heat for 2-3 minutes.

Stir gently once, cover with a tight-fitting lid, reduce heat to very low and cook for a further 10-12 minutes. Remove pan from heat, leave covered and undisturbed for a further 5 minutes. Turn out rice into a serving dish and garnish with the remaining nuts, and the silver leaves if you're using them.

Handy Hints
1. An additional garnish: Use finely sliced and crisply fried onion rings and potato fingers.
2. One or two tablespoonfuls of fried raisins can be substituted for the above.

PURI
deep fried wholemeal bread

YOU WILL NEED

4 oz (100 g) wholewheat flour

4 oz (100 g) plain flour

1 tsp melted ghee

pinch salt

4-5 fl oz (120-150 ml) water, to make a stiff dough vegetable oil for deep frying

dry flour for dusting when rolling out

Puri, the commonest type of deep fried bread is eaten throughout India and is a great favourite, no matter what the occasion. A professional cook can easily fry a dozen or more puris in a single batch in less than a couple of minutes!

Sieve the wholemeal and plain flours together with the salt.

Make a stiff but pliable dough with sufficient water. With the ghee added at intervals, knead for about 10 minutes. Leave it covered with a damp cloth for 15-20 minutes.

Knead lightly again and divide the dough into 16 parts. Taking each part in turn shape it into a ball and then flatten it between the palms; dust it with dry flour and keep aside. Then roll it out (with the help of a little dry flour) into a thin puri (pancake) about 3 inches (8 cm) in diameter.

Heat the vegetable oil in a kadhai to near smoking point and fry the puris one at a time on medium heat, pressing it down with a flat perforated spoon till it swells up. (This takes a few seconds only.) Turn it over, and cook the second side for a little longer until it is also lightly browned. Remove from oil, drain on kitchen paper and serve hot.

Puris are at their best when eaten hot and crisp—as soon as they are fried. However, even if they lose their crispness when cold, they are still quite tasty.

Handy Hint

The dough can be made more effortlessly and quickly in a food processor by processing all the ingredients together and using just sufficient water as required for a stiff, pliable dough.

DOUBLE KA MITHA
bread and milk pudding

YOU WILL NEED

12 slices (medium) white bread, preferably a day or two old

1³/₄ pints (1 litre) milk

¹/₄ pint (300 ml) sweetened condensed milk

6 green cardamoms (shelled and crushed)

few drops rose essence *or* 1 tbsp rose water

2 tbsp sultanas

2 tbsp coarsely chopped almonds with their skins

2 tbsp coarsely chopped cashewnuts

vegetable oil for deep frying

We feel this is one of the nicest and tastiest of Indian puddings. Don't let its simple ingredients put you off—it truly gives a 'grand' result with very little effort.

Cut bread slices diagonally into halves and deep fry on medium heat in batches until crisp and deep golden in colour. Remove and keep aside.

In the same oil fry lightly the almonds and cashewnuts. Drain well and keep aside.

Bring the milk to boil. Lower heat and slowly add condensed milk to it. Let the mixture simmer for 1-2 minutes. Add the fried bread pieces—gently mixing them and soaking them completely in the milk mixture. Add crushed cardamoms, rose essence and the sultanas. Stir occasionally, but very slowly and with care—as it is nice for the pieces to retain their shape. Cook on medium heat until the bread soaks up all the liquid and acquires a semi-dry appearance.

Remove from heat, transfer to a serving dish and garnish with fried almonds and cashewnuts. Serve hot or cold.

Handy Hint
A chocolate flavour can be produced by adding 1 tablespoonful of cocoa powder along with the milk mixture before adding the fried bread. Try it—it makes a lovely change!

JAL ZEERA
an appetizing aromatic drink

YOU WILL NEED

2 oz (50 g) fresh mint leaves

4 oz (115 g) dried mango powder *or* 2 oz (50 g) tamarind paste

2 tsp black cumin seeds

1 tsp salt, or to taste

$1/2$ tsp black salt (optional)

$1/2$ tsp freshly ground black peppercorns

1 tbsp brown sugar or molasses

1 tbsp fresh ginger, grated and peeled

3 $1/4$ pints (2 litres) cold water

ice cubes

A very different kind of a thirst quencher indeed! Although more of an appetizer, it can easily be served along with the main meal.

Mix the mango powder/tamarind paste, salts, pepper and molasses. Add to the water and leave to stand for at least half an hour. Grind the mint leaves and ginger to a thick paste form and add this to the water. Stand again for at least half an hour. Strain through a coarse muslin cloth. Serve with ice-cubes and a sprig of mint floating on the top.

Handy Hint

To vary the taste according to your needs, alter the proportions of salt, pepper and molasses. If desired, a little chilli powder or 2-3 cloves can be added as well.

Elaborate Dinner for Non-Vegetarians

ANOKHA CHICKEN
*Pan-Fried Chicken with
a Difference*

MUGHLAI KHORMA
*A Rich and Spicy
Lamb Curry*

DALCHA
*Pulses and Meat
Curry*

PALAK-ALOO-KI BHAJI
*Dry Potatoes with
Spinach*

PUDINE KA RAITA
Yoghurt with Mint

HARA SALAD
*Green Salad
(For details see page 74)*

YAKHNI PULAO
Rice Cooked in Lamb Broth

TANDOORI ROTI
Grilled Wholemeal Bread

SEVIYAN ZARDA
Vermicelli Pudding

NIMBU PAANI
*Fresh Lime Drink
(For details see page 50)*

Serves six to eight people

ANOKHA CHICKEN
pan-fried chicken with a difference

YOU WILL NEED

2¼ lbs (1 kg) boneless, skinless chicken

FOR THE MARINADE

2 tsp garam masala

2 tsp red chilli powder (medium hot)

2 tsp salt, or to taste

2 tsp ginger puree

2 tsp garlic puree

½ tsp (tomato) food colour

3 tbsp natural yoghurt

2 tsp malt vinegar

oil for deep frying

2 large eggs

4 tbsp cornflour

FOR SEASONING

2 tbsp oil/ghee

8 tbsp fresh coriander leaves, chopped

2 tbsp green chillies, chopped

4 tbsp natural yoghurt

4 tbsp tomato or chilli sauce

2 tbsp finely chopped ginger

2 tbsp finely chopped garlic

a few curry leaves (carripatta)

This very unusual recipe will never fail to please. It is versatile as it can be served either as a snack or as part of a main meal.

Mix all ingredients for marinading. Add chicken pieces and leave covered in the fridge for at lest 5-6 hours.

Add two lightly beaten eggs and cornflour to chicken. Mix gently together.

Heat oil and on medium heat, fry all the chicken pieces (in batches), until a nice golden colour is obtained—do not brown the pieces. Remove, drain and keep aside.

Seasoning: In another pan, heat oil/ghee. Add ginger, curry leaves, green coriander and chillies and stir for just 30-40 seconds—then add yoghurt, tomato/chilli sauce and a little salt if needed. Stir for a few seconds only, add fried chicken; stir quickly and serve the chicken while it is sizzling hot.

Handy Hints

1. The chicken can be served as a snack prior to seasoning it.

2. Adding finely sliced onions to the seasoning makes a welcome change.

MUGHLAI KHORMA
a rich spicy lamb curry

YOU WILL NEED

2 lbs (900g) lean lamb, cut into 1$\frac{1}{2}$" (4 cm) pieces

FOR THE MARINADE

2 oz (60 g) onions, peeled and roughly chopped

1 oz (30 g) fresh ginger, scraped

4-6 cloves garlic, peeled

1 tsp salt

1 tbsp coriander seeds, dry roasted and powdered

FOR THE GRAVY

4 oz (120 g) ghee (not cooking oil)

4 oz (120 g) onions, peeled and sliced

1 tsp red chilli powder

1 tsp salt

6 fl oz (180 ml) natural yoghurt

5 fl oz (150 ml) double cream

large pinch saffron, dissolved in 1 tbsp hot water

1 tbsp powdered cashewnuts

1 tbsp almond powder

1 tsp garam masala powder

1 tsp rose water

10 fl oz (300 ml) hot water

This preparation has its origins in the courts of the Moghuls who were renowned for their rich and sumptuous cuisine.

The addition of nuts and cream to the gravy gives it a unique and superb taste.

Liquidize all the above ingredients for the marinade. Coat the lamb pieces with this mixture and leave for 2-3 hours in a cool place.

Heat ghee in a heavy-based saucepan and fry the onions until golden brown. Remove them, grind to a paste and keep them aside.

Re-heat the same ghee, add red chilli powder and sprinkle a tablespoon of hot water to prevent it from burning. After a few seconds add the marinaded meat and salt. Stir and fry until all the liquid released from the meat is re-absorbed. Add hot water, cover and simmer on low heat until the lamb is tender.

Stir in the beaten yoghurt and mix well. After a few minutes add the fried ground onions followed a couple of minutes later by the cream, saffron, cashewnut and almond powders. Mix well, sprinkle the garam masala powder, cover pan and continue cooking on very low heat for a further few minutes.

Remove from heat and add a few drops of rose water. Serve hot.

Handy Hint
Use chicken instead of lamb but reduce the amount of water as well as the cooking time.

DALCHA
pulses and meat curry

YOU WILL NEED

6 oz (170 g) yellow split lentils, without skin

1 tsp red chilli powder

1 tsp turmeric powder

2 fl oz (150 ml) cooking oil

1 tsp black cumin seeds

2-3 cloves

4 oz (115 g) onions, sliced

1 tsp fresh ginger, grated

1 tsp crushed garlic

4 oz (115 g) breast of lamb, trimmed and cut into pieces

1 ¹/₂ tsp salt, or to taste

5 fl oz (150 ml) water for cooking the lamb

1 oz (30 g) tamarind pods soaked in 1 cup water and juice extracted

There are innumerable ways of cooking lentils—on their own, with vegetables or with meat. The special feature of dalcha is that it combines pulses with meat.

Clean and wash the lentils thoroughly and put them to boil along with the red chilli and turmeric powders and cook until soft. Keep aside.

Meanwhile, set a heavy pan with the cooking oil on medium heat, and when hot, add cumin seeds and cloves. After a few seconds, add sliced onions and fry until golden brown. Then add the ginger and garlic and stir and fry for a few seconds before adding the meat. Continue stirring and frying the meat until it is nicely browned and oil begins to separate. Add salt and water. Cover and cook until the meat is tender. (Use a little more water if necessary.)

Combine the cooked meat with the cooked lentils and add the extracted juice of tamarind. Cover and bring to boil. Lower heat and simmer gently for approximately 5 minutes. Keep the dalcha covered and warm, ready for the final seasoning.

For final seasoning ('baghar')
Heat the ghee in a small saucepan, add whole red chillies, curry leaves, fenugreek and cumin seeds. Fry until the seeds begin to splutter. Pour this ghee mixture immediately over the cooked dalcha and cover with a tight-fitting lid. Leave it to stand undisturbed for 1-2 minutes for the flavours to infuse. Remember to remove the whole red chillies before eating.

82

Contd. ....

30 fl oz (900 ml) water
for cooking lentils

FINAL SEASONING

1 oz (30 g) ghee

2 whole red chillies

10-12 curry leaves

¹/₂ tsp cumin seeds

3-4 grains fenugreek seeds

Handy Hint
Bengal gram or split red lentils may be substituted
for yellow split lentils.

PALAK-ALOO-KI BHAJI
dry potatoes with spinach

YOU WILL NEED

8 oz (225 g) potatoes

8 oz (225 g) spinach

4 tbsp vegetable cooking oil

1-2 whole red chillies

4-6 grains fenugreek seeds

4 oz (115 g) onions, peeled and sliced

1 tsp salt

$\frac{1}{4}$ tsp red chilli powder

$\frac{1}{4}$ tsp turmeric powder

1 tomato, chopped

A good variety of green leafy vegetables which are both cheap and plentiful is available all year round in the Indian marketplace. Each variety has its own different flavour and spinach is specially popular.

Greens are also a good source of minerals and fibre, with spinach being particularly rich in iron. In this simple recipe, spinach lends a distinctive flavour to the potatoes.

Peel and cut the potatoes into 1" (2.5 cm) cubes. Wash the spinach thoroughly, and chop it roughly.

In a saucepan, heat oil and saute the potatoes until golden. Remove potatoes and keep aside.

Re-heat the same oil, add whole red chillies and fenugreek seeds. Stir and fry for a few seconds and then add sliced onions.

Fry the onions until light brown in colour and add the red chilli and turmeric powders. Immediately remove the pan from heat, add 1 tbsp water, stir and return the pan to heat. Add tomatoes and fry until they are soft. Add spinach and stir. Cover and cook for a further 5-7 minutes approximately or until the potatoes are tender. If any liquid remains, uncover pan and dry it off.

Handy Hints
1. To vary: Use 4 oz (115 g) of skinned fried peanuts instead of potatoes. Follow recipe as above.

2. A pinch of powdered mace may be added for improved flavour.

PUDINE KA RAITA
yoghurt with mint

YOU WILL NEED

10 fl oz (150 ml) thick set natural yoghurt

4 tbsp fresh mint leaves

1 tsp salt

$^1/_2$ tsp freshly milled black pepper

You will be hard put to find a more instant and flavourful raita than this one.

Blend all the ingredients in a liquidizer. Pour into a bowl. Chill, and serve garnished with a couple of fresh mint leaves.

HARA SALAAD
green salad

(For details see page 74)

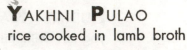

YAKHNI PULAO
rice cooked in lamb broth

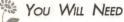

YOU WILL NEED

a piece of clean muslin
6" x 6" (15 x 15 cm)
approximately

FOR YAKHNI OR BROTH

1 ¹/₂ lb (675 g) leg of
lamb pieces on bone, cut
into medium size

2 oz (60 g) onions, chopped

2-3 green chillies, chopped

4 cloves garlic, peeled

2" piece ginger, peeled
and sliced

2" piece cinnamon

6 cloves

1 tsp coriander seeds

1 tsp salt

2 pints (1.3 litres) water

FOR THE PULAO

10 oz (275 g) Basmati rice

Yakhni pulao is rice cooked in a rich lamb broth. The broth which gives this pulao a special flavour is prepared by cooking the lamb with spices which are tied in a muslin bag and later discarded.

Method for Yakhni
Wash the lamb and put it in a large pan. Loosely tie all the remaining ingredients from onion to salt in the muslin square.

Place this muslin bag in the above pan together with the water. Bring it to boil. Cover pan and allow contents to simmer gently on low heat until the lamb is almost done. Remove the pan from heat, discard the muslin bag, and remove the lamb pieces with a slotted spoon. Keep these aside. You should now be left with approximately 4 cups of broth.

Method for making the pulao
Wash and drain the rice through a sieve.

Grind the ginger and garlic to a fine paste. Heat the cooking oil in a large heavy-based pan and fry the onions to a rich golden brown colour. Remove half the onions and keep them aside for garnishing later.

To the remaining onions in the pan, add the ginger-garlic paste and all the dry spices. Fry for 1-2 minutes. Now add the lamb pieces and fry them to a nice brown colour. Whilst frying the lamb, stir in a few tablespoons of yoghurt at a time until all the yoghurt is used up. Now add the drained rice to the meat and fry gently for a further 2-3 minutes. Add salt and the remaining broth and bring to boil. Cover

Contd. ....

2 cloves garlic, peeled

1" (2.5 cm) piece ginger, peeled

3 fl oz (80 ml) vegetable cooking oil

4 oz (115 g) onions, peeled and cut into fine rings

$\frac{1}{2}$ tsp black cumin seeds

1" (2.5 cm) piece cinnamon

2-3 green cardamoms

4 cloves

1 tsp salt

4 fl oz (115 ml) natural yoghurt

3 fl oz (80 ml) vegetable cooking oil

FOR GARNISH

2-3 hard-boiled eggs/ sliced

with a tight-fitting lid, reduce heat to very low and cook for another 10-15 minutes.

Serve hot, garnished with the reserved onion rings and sliced hard-boiled eggs.

TANDOORI ROTI
grilled wholemeal bread

YOU WILL NEED

1 lb (450 g) wholewheat flour

7 fl oz (210 ml) water (approximately)

melted ghee or butter for brushing over

Tandoori roti derives its name from the word tandoor, the clay oven in which it is baked.

In the Punjab, it is common practice for the housewife to send her own dough to the corner tandoori stall-holder who will happily bake the rotis for her at a minimal charge.

Here we are showing an alternative method for making the rotis without a tandoor.

Sift the flour into a large bowl and add sufficient water to make a pliable dough which should be soft but not sticky. Knead for a few minutes until the texture is smooth. Cover with a damp cloth and leave aside for half an hour or so.

Knead the dough again for a minute or two before dividing it into 8-10 equal balls.

Pre-heat the grill to a high setting and place a heavy griddle on medium heat.

Dust each ball of dough with dry flour, flatten and roll out fairly thickly ($\frac{1}{4}$" thickness 7-8 mm approximately). Brush lightly with water and place the moistened side on the griddle. Let the roti cook until the edges begin to lift a little and some bubbles appear on the surface. Check the underside to see if it has turned slightly brown. Remove carefully with a spatula and place the uncooked surface on a tray under a hot grill. As soon as the roti begins to swell and acquires a few brown spots remove from the grill. Smear a little melted ghee or butter and keep it warm by wrapping it in a tea towel. Cook all the remaining dough in the same way.

Tandoori roti is best served as soon as it is made. If, however, it needs to be re-heated, wrap it in aluminium foil and place in a hot oven for a few minutes.

SEVIYAN ZARDA
vermicelli pudding

Vermicelli is in itself a versatile ingredient, but is almost always turned into a sweetmeat or dessert in India. This seviyan zarda is associated with most Muslim festivals.

YOU WILL NEED

2 oz (60 g) ghee

4 green cardamoms, crushed

2 cloves

6 oz (170 g) very fine quality vermicelli

30 fl oz (900 ml) full cream milk

6 oz (170 g) sugar

pinch saffron

1 tbsp rose water

1 oz (30 g) almonds, slivered

1 oz (30 g) pistachios, slivered

silver leaves

Heat the ghee in a large saucepan, add the crushed cardamoms and cloves and after a few seconds add the vermicelli. Fry on low heat, stirring gently until it is a rich golden brown colour. Pour in the milk. Increase the heat to medium, and bring to boil. Continue cooking, stirring occasionally until about half the milk remains.

Add the sugar, stir it in well, and cook again until the pudding has thickened in consistency.

Dissolve the saffron in rose water and sprinkle over the seviyan. Turn it out into a serving bowl and decorate with slivered almonds, pistachio nuts and silver leaves.

Serve hot or cold.

NIMBU PAANI
fresh lime drink

(For details see page 50)

Celebration Dinner for Vegetarians

PALAK AUR BADAAM KA SOUP
Spinach and Almond Soup

SABUDANA AUR MOONGPHALLI KE VADE
Sago and Nut Cutlets

SHAHI KAJU KA KHORMA
Rich Cashewnut Curry

BHARWAN TANDOORI PANEER
Stuffed Tandoori Cottage Cheese

DUM KI SAABUT GOBHI
Whole Cauliflower Baked

LOBHIA
Butter-Beans Curry

LAUKI KA RAITA
Yoghurt with White Gourd

HARE DHANIE KI CHUTNEY
Fresh Green Coriander Chutney

MILI JULI SABZION KA ACHAAR
Mixed Vegetable Pickle

MATAR PULAO
Peas Pulao

ROGHNI ROTI
Enriched Bread

GAJAR KA HALWA
Carrot Pudding

BADAAM KI BARFI
Almond Fudge

NAMKEEN LASSI
Savoury Butter milk

Serves twelve to fourteen people

PALAK AUR BADAAM KA SOUP
spinach and almond soup

YOU WILL NEED

4 oz (130 g) fresh spinach or chopped frozen spinach

1 tbsp butter

1 oz (30 g) onions, peeled and chopped

$^1/_2$ tsp salt, or to taste

$^1/_4$ tsp sugar

10 fl oz (300 ml) water

pinch cumin seeds, crushed

pinch nutmeg

1 oz (30 g) almond powder

5 fl oz (150 ml) full cream milk, warmed

4 tbsp double cream

Soups as such do not constitute any real part of a traditional Indian meal, but have crept into the cuisine as a result of Western influences. This particular soup is a good example of how they have been adapted and become Indianised in turn.

Because of their high nutritive value and easy digestibility, soups tend to be served mostly to convalescents and the elderly—but may occasionally be served along with the main meal.

Wash the fresh spinach leaves thoroughly (if using frozen, defrost) and liquidize.

Melt the butter in a saucepan, add cumin seeds and saute onions. Add salt, sugar and pureed spinach. Stir and cook for 4-5 minutes. Then add the water, bring it to a boil and let it simmer on medium heat for about 5 minutes. Rub through a sieve and keep aside.

Just before serving, add a pinch of nutmeg, almond powder, hot milk and 3 tbsp cream. Stir and let it simmer gently for 2-3 minutes. Check the consistency of the soup and if it looks too thick, add a little more milk. Garnish with a tablespoonful of double cream.

Handy Hint
If a less rich soup is required, omit the double cream and serve with croutons if so desired.

SABUDANA AUR MOONGPHALLI KE VADE
sago and nut cutlets

YOU WILL NEED

10 oz (300 g) potatoes, boiled and mashed thoroughly

4 oz (115 g) sago

4 oz (115 g) unsalted groundnuts, roasted and coarsely crushed

2-3 green chillies, or to taste, finely chopped

2 tbsp green coriander leaves, finely chopped

1 $\frac{1}{4}$ tsp salt, or to taste

1 tsp lemon juice

1 tsp dry roasted cumin seeds, powdered

vegetable cooking oil for deep frying

Nuts and cereals combined together play an important part in making well balanced and satisfying vegetarian meals. The vegetarians from the Western Ghat area have devised this pleasing combination of sago and peanuts in the shape of these tasty cutlets.

Wash and soak sago in sufficient cold water to cover it. Leave aside for 15 minutes.

By this time, most of the water should have been absorbed, but if any remains, drain it away. Except for the cooking oil, mix all the ingredients gently together—do not rub or mash them.

Divide into 10 or 12 equal portions. Press each portion gently between the palms to form into a round shape.

Heat the cooking oil in a kadhai or deep frying pan set on medium heat, and when hot, deep fry cutlets in 2 or 3 batches until golden brown. Drain on absorbent kitchen paper. Serve hot.

Handy Hint

If sago is not at hand, add 4 slices of white bread instead. The slices must first be moistened with a little water and then crumbled roughly.

SHAHI KAJU KA KHORMA
rich cashewnut curry

YOU WILL NEED

1 lb (450 g) whole cashewnuts

1 ¹/₂" (4 cm) root ginger, peeled

4 cloves garlic

¹/₂ tsp black cumin seeds

2 green cardamoms

1" (2.5 cm) cinnamon

4 cloves

4 peppercorns

¹/₂ tsp saffron

¹/₂ tsp chilli powder

2 fl oz (60 ml) ghee

4 oz (115 g) onions, peeled and grated

1 tsp salt, or to taste

4 tbsp natural yoghurt

2 tbsp poppy seeds, dry roasted and powdered

Most Indian cooks do not look upon the task of providing wholesome yet tasty vegetarian dishes for all sorts of different occasions as particularly challenging. This is largely due to the long and ancient tradition of vegetarianism in India.

The following recipe is unique because it uses cashewnuts in place of vegetables to make a rich and mouthwatering vegetarian dish.

Soak the cashewnuts in sufficient hot water to cover them. Leave for 10-15 minutes. Drain and keep aside.

Grind ginger, garlic and black cumin seeds to a paste.

Grind the cardamoms, cinnamon, cloves and peppercorns into a coarse powder.

Gently heat saffron in a tablespoon for a few seconds. Crush and soak it in 2 tablespoonfuls of hot milk.

Heat ghee in a heavy-based pan set on medium heat, and fry the grated onions until golden brown. Add the coarsely powdered spices and fry for a few seconds. Then add the ginger-garlic and cumin seed paste and stir and fry for a minute or so. Sprinkle a little water and stir until the water is absorbed. This prevents the mixture from sticking and burning and helps it to fry evenly. Add salt, chilli powder and beaten yoghurt and keep stirring and frying until all the liquid is absorbed and ghee begins to separate and float on top.

Contd. ....

2 tbsp double cream

5 fl oz (150 ml) hot water

Add the soaked and dried cashewnuts, fry for 2-3 minutes and then add the powdered poppy seeds and continue frying for a few more seconds. Now add half a cup of hot water. Cover and cook on low heat for about 5 minutes. Lastly add the cream and mix well. Check the sauce—if too thick add a little more hot water. Cover and continue cooking on low heat for a further 3-4 minutes.

Handy Hint

As cashewnuts are expensive, this dish may be stretched further with the addition of 4 oz (115 g) green peas.

Bharwan Tandoori Paneer
stuffed tandoori cottage cheese

You Will Need

1¹/₂ lb (700 g) slab of cottage cheese

6 tbsp hare dhanie ki chutney (see Page 48)

3 tbsp tandoori masala powder

6 tbsp natural yoghurt

3 tbsp oil/ghee for brushing over

3 tbsp mixed amchur and dry roasted powdered cumin seeds

6 green chillies, slit lengthwise, for garnish

This recipe is unusual because the paneer is baked rather than fried. The finished dish looks as good as it tastes.

Cut the paneer slab crosswise into three layers. Sandwich the layers with chutney.

In an oven-proof dish smear a little ghee and place the paneer slab in it.

Mix tandoori powder with yoghurt and apply it all over the paneer covering the slab completely. Leave it for 15 minutes.

Brush a little oil/ghee on top, cover and bake in a very hot oven for approximately 10 minutes. Uncover and bake for a further 5 minutes, ideally just before serving.

Sprinkle *amchur* and powdered roasted cumin seeds. The paneer looks good with sliced green chillies around it. Cut it into wedges and serve hot.

Handy Hint
Other chutneys e.g., coconut, peanut, etc., can be substituted to produce a variety in taste.

DUM KI SAABUT GOBHI
whole cauliflower baked

YOU WILL NEED

1 medium sized cauliflower head approximately 1¹/² lb (680 g), left whole

4 fl oz (120 ml) ghee, preferably

2 cloves garlic

1" (2.5 cm) root ginger

2 green chillies

3 oz (90 g) onions, peeled and grated

1 tsp coriander powder

¹/₂ tsp red chilli powder

¹/₄ tsp turmeric powder

1 tsp salt, or to taste

2 tbsp tomato puree or fresh tomatoes, pureed

5 fl oz (150 ml) hot water

¹/₂ tsp garam masala powder

1 tbsp green coriander leaves, finely chopped

This baked dish is exceedingly presentable and delectable—ideal for parties.

Pre-heat oven to medium setting.

Remove the outer leaves and stalk from the cauliflower; wash and dry the head. Heat ghee in a kadhai or deep frying pan set on medium heat and fry the inverted head of the cauliflower until lightly browned. Remove and keep aside.

Grind together the ginger, garlic and green chillies.

Re-heat the remaining ghee and fry the grated onions until golden brown. Add the ground ginger-garlic-green chilli paste and fry for a minute or so, sprinkling a little water as necessary to prevent the mixture from sticking to the bottom of the pan.

Add the turmeric, chilli and coriander powders and salt. Fry for a few seconds and then add the tomato puree. Continue stirring and frying for another minute or so then add the hot water. Reduce heat, cover pan and cook for 3-4 minutes. The masala (sauce) should now be of pouring consistency. If it is too dry, add a little more hot water and allow it to simmer for 2-3 minutes.

Take a baking dish just large enough to hold the cauliflower. Place the cauliflower upright in it and pour the prepared masala (sauce) over it, ensuring that some masala goes into the cavities of the cauliflower as well. Sprinkle garam masala powder, cover and bake in a pre-heated oven for approximately 20 minutes or until the cauliflower is

Contd. ....

tender, but does not begin to break up.

Before serving, spoon the masala from the bottom of the baking dish over the top of the cauliflower and sprinkle with fresh green coriander leaves.

Handy Hint
The flavour of pure ghee is unbeatable; but for the more health conscious, a half and half mixture of ghee and vegetable cooking oil is recommended.

LOBHIA
butter-beans curry

Lobhia which belongs to the kidney bean family is cooked in a similar manner to rajmah (red kidney beans). However, it produces an entirely different flavour and has a much creamier taste and texture.

YOU WILL NEED

FOR COOKING THE BEANS

1 lb (450 g) butter beans

3 pints (1.8 litres) water

1/2 tsp turmeric powder

1/2 tsp chilli powder

1 tbsp salt

FOR THE SAUCE

3 oz (85 g) ghee

4 cloves

1" (2.5 cm) cinnamon

4 oz (115 g) onions

2 oz (60 g) ginger, peeled and grated

2 cloves garlic, crushed

2 oz (60 g) chopped fresh tomatoes

4 fl oz (115 ml) natural yoghurt, beaten

few coriander leaves for garnish

For cooking beans
Follow the recipe as for rajmah (Page 32)

For the sauce
Heat ghee in a saucepan and add the whole cloves and cinnamon. When they begin to swell, add the onions and fry until they turn pinkish. Then add the ginger and garlic and stir and fry until golden brown. Next add the chopped tomatoes and continue stirring and frying until the tomatoes are soft. Now add the beaten yoghurt a little at a time and fry for another few minutes until all the yoghurt is absorbed and ghee separates from the mixture.

Add the cooked butter beans along with their cooking liquid and mix well. If the consistency is too thick, add a little more boiling water. Cover and cook on low heat for a further 5-10 minutes. Sprinkle coriander leaves and serve.

Handy Hint
Butter beans can be cooked well in advance and frozen without any loss of taste. Simply defrost, re-heat thoroughly and serve with a little garnish of fresh coriander leaves.

LAUKI KA RAITA
yoghurt with white gourd

YOU WILL NEED

10 fl oz (285 ml) natural yoghurt

6 oz (175 g) white gourd

1/4 tsp salt, or to taste

pinch chilli powder

1/4 tsp cumin seeds, dry roasted and powdered

This is a very mild and pleasant accompaniment to any Indian meal.

Peel the white gourd; remove and discard the large seeds. Grate the remaining gourd coarsely.

Put the grated gourd into a bowl and pour sufficient boiling water over it to cover it completely. Allow it to stand for approximately 5 minutes. (If the gourd is really young and tender, it should get done within this time, but if it is tough, steam it a little longer.) Drain and squeeze out the extra moisture. Allow to cool.

Put the yoghurt in a serving bowl and whisk along with the salt and roasted cumin powder until smooth and creamy. Gently stir in the grated gourd and sprinkle with chilli powder.

HARE DHANIA KI CHUTNEY
fresh green coriander chutney

YOU WILL NEED

4 oz (115 g) fresh green coriander leaves, washed

3-4 green chillies, or less for a milder chutney

1 tsp salt

1 tsp sugar

1 tbsp lemon juice, preferably freshly squeezed

2 tbsp water

This refreshing chutney is ideal for those who appreciate the distinctive fragrance of green coriander leaves. What is better, it can be prepared in next to no time.

Mix all the ingredients together and liquidize. The chutney will keep well for 3-4 days in the fridge.

MILI JULI SABZION KA KHATTA-MITHA ACHAAR
sweet and sour mixed vegetable pickle

YOU WILL NEED

2 lbs (900 g) turnips

2 lbs (900 g) cauliflower

1 lb (450 g) carrots

5 oz (150 g) ginger

5 oz (150 g) garlic

1 1/4 pint (750 ml) mustard oil

2-3 bay leaves

6 oz (175 g) small yellow mustard seeds, ground

3 oz (75 g) salt

2 oz (50 g) chilli powder

1 tsp black cumin seeds

1 tsp nutmeg, ground

12 fl oz (325 ml) malt vinegar

1 1/2 lb (225 g) dark brown sugar or molasses

1 oz (25 g) garam masala powder

1/2 tsp red colouring

Pickles can be mild or extremely hot. They can also be either sweet or sour or a combination of both. This sweet and sour mixed vegetable pickle is a great favourite amongst the Northerners, so much so that sometimes it is substituted as a side vegetable dish.

Wash and chop the vegetables into a minimum of 2" (5 cm) pieces; spread them out on a tea towel and leave to dry overnight.

Grind the ginger and garlic into a paste without adding any water. In a large saucepan, heat oil to smoking point.

Remove from heat and allow to cool slightly. Then add the bay leaves and the ground ginger-garlic paste and fry for a few seconds until golden brown.

Return pan to heat, add the vegetables and fry until they are just slightly cooked. Then add the ground mustard, salt, chilli powder and black cumin seeds, nutmeg and garam masala powder. Mix the vegetables thoroughly and leave to cool.

Take another saucepan (non-aluminium, preferably stainless steel), heat the vinegar in it, and add the brown sugar. Bring it to a boil. Allow this syrup to cool and pour it over the vegetables.

Put the pickle into a sterilized jar, cover and leave it in a warm place or in the sun. This pickle will mature in about three weeks' time, and keeps well even upto a year. However, some people like to start eating it within a week when it is more akin to spiced vegetables.

MATAR PULAO
peas pulao

You Will Need

9 oz (250 g) Basmati rice

16 fl oz (450 ml) warm water

3 oz (90 g) ghee

1" (2.5 cm) cinnamon

6 peppercorns

1 tsp cumin seeds

2-3 green cardamoms

3 oz (90 g) onions, peeled and finely sliced

2 green chillies

4 oz (120 g) shelled peas

1/2 tsp chilli powder

1 tsp garam masala

1 tsp salt

Of all the pulaos, matar pulao is perhaps the one that is the most commonly served, especially for vegetarians. It looks good, tastes good and does not require much time or effort in its preparation.

Clean and wash the rice in several changes of water, rubbing the rice very gently between the fingers until the water runs clear.

Drain the rice through a sieve. Soak it in the measured amount of water for 15-20 minutes. Then drain the rice as before, but remember to save the water for cooking the rice later on.

Heat the ghee in a heavy-based pan set on medium heat. Add the cinnamon, peppercorns, cumin seeds and cardamoms. After a few seconds, add the onions and green chillies. Fry until the onions are golden brown. Then add the peas, chilli and garam masala powders and stir and fry for another 5 minutes or so.

Next add the drained rice, mix gently and fry for a few minutes until all the grains are well coated with ghee. Add salt and the reserved water. Increase the heat and bring the rice to boil rapidly for 2-3 minutes. Then cover the pan with a tight-fitting lid, reduce heat to very low and leave the rice undisturbed for 10-12 minutes.

Remove the pan from the heat, but do not uncover the lid for a further 5 minutes. Serve hot.

ROGHNI ROTI
enriched unleavened bread

YOU WILL NEED

1 lb (450 g) plain flour

$^1/_2$ tsp salt

3 oz (85 g) ghee plus a little extra for rubbing over the cooked roti

$^1/_2$ pint (280 ml) milk + water (half & half)

This delicious unleavened bread remains soft and fresh tasting even when stored for 2-3 days. It tastes quite good even when eaten cold with pickle for breakfast.

Special Requirement
A griddle

Sift the flour along with the salt. Rub in the melted ghee and knead to a soft dough with the milk and water mixture.

Divide the dough into 10-12 equal portions. Shape each portion into a round, smooth ball and roll it out into a roti (i.e., like a pancake) of $^1/_8$" (0.5 cm) thickness.

Set the griddle on medium heat and place the rolled out roti on it. Lower the heat just a little, place the rolled out roti on the griddle and cook until the underside has a few brown spots. With the help of a spatula turn the roti over and let the second side cook in the same way.

Remove the roti from the griddle. Brush with a little melted ghee, and fold into quarters. Cook all rotis in this way, stack and keep them wrapped in a tea towel.

Serve immediately. If that is not possible, make the rotis in advance, wrap them in cooking foil and warm them up in a hot oven for just a few minutes. Alternatively, these rotis may also be served without being re-heated if so desired.

Handy Hint
If a microwave oven is handy, roghni rotis can be re-heated beautifully within 20-30 seconds on high power.

GAJAR KA HALWA
carrot pudding

YOU WILL NEED

1 lb (450 g) carrots

4 tbsp pure ghee

12 fl oz (360 ml) milk

3 oz (85 g) sugar

6 oz (170 g) paneer

pinch saffron or orange
food colouring (optional)
dissolved in 1 tbsp water

3-4 green cardamoms,
shelled and seeds
powdered

1 oz (30 g) unsalted
pistachio nuts

2 oz (60 g) almonds,
blanched and sliced

silver leaves (optional)

This is one of the choicest of all the halwas, and can do honour to any occasion! It is generally associated with the cold winter months, when carrots are abundant. A plateful of warmed up halwa can prove quite irresistible, both for adults as well as children.

Wash, scrape and shred/grate carrots finely.

Heat ghee in a heavy-based pan and fry the grated carrots for 5 minutes, then reduce heat, cover and cook for about 10 minutes, or until carrots are tender. (The carrots will cook in their own juices.) Add milk and cook uncovered on high heat, stirring frequently until the milk is completely absorbed and the halwa is nearly dry.

Now add the sugar, and stir till it dissolves. Continue cooking further so that the mixture becomes dry once again. Add the crumbled paneer along with the dissolved saffron or food colouring, mix thoroughly and stir-fry for 5 minutes. Remove from heat and stir in half of the nuts and powdered cardamom seeds. Spoon out halwa on to a serving dish, garnish with silver leaves (if using) and sprinkle remaining nuts over it.

Handy Hint
To give a slightly different flavour, omit cardamoms. When halwa is cooked and ready, sprinkle a few drops of rose water over it.

Gajar-ka-halwa can be heated successfully in a microwave oven.

Caution
Do *not* use silver leaves prior to heating in a microwave.

BADAAM KI BARFI
almond fudge

YOU WILL NEED

3/4 pint (425 ml) full cream milk

4 oz (115 g) ground almond powder

4 oz (115 g) sugar

2 oz (60 g) full cream milk powder

2 green cardamoms, peeled and crushed

2 dozen blanched almonds, slivered

Most Indians love sweets! Barfi is one of the most popular and commonly made sweetmeats. Perhaps the nearest equivalent to barfi is fudge, in that they are both milk-based and require fair amounts of sugar. Like most other Indian sweetmeats, barfi can be served as a dessert or as a tea time snack.

In a heavy-based pan, boil the milk. Add the ground almond powder and boil quickly till mixture thickens (approximately 15-20 minutes.) Stir frequently to prevent it from sticking.

Add the milk powder, sugar, and cardamoms and stirring continuously cook for a further 5-6 minutes, or till the mixture is fairly stiff (almost like a soft dough) and begins to leave the sides of the pan.

Spread mixture on a pre-greased dish with slightly raised edges, and decorate with blanched and slivered almonds.

When cool and set, cut into diamond shapes. Store in an air-tight container. It will keep in the fridge for a week or so.

Handy Hint
To vary, use chopped pistachio nuts instead of slivered almonds.

NAMKEEN LASSI
savoury buttermilk

YOU WILL NEED

5 fl oz (180 ml) natural yoghurt

1 1/4 pints (750 ml) cold water

1/4 tsp salt, or to taste

10 -12 (300 ml) ice cubes

pinch freshly milled black pepper

Lassi is an age-old beverage of India which has stood the test of time, and has only recently been introduced as a healthy yoghurt drink to the West. It is cooling and light, and may be served with a meal or on its own at any time as a thirst quencher.

Whisk together the yoghurt, salt and pepper. Add cold water and whisk again. Check seasoning—it should have the merest hint of a savoury taste. Pour the lassi in a jug and serve chilled with ice cubes.

Handy Hints
1. If serving lassi on its own (not with a meal), a pinch of rock salt and a garnish of 3-4 mint leaves will give it a delightful flavour.

2. To vary the flavour, add a large pinch of dry roasted and powdered cumin seeds and 4-5 finely chopped mint leaves to the basic recipe given above. Makes a very refreshing drink.

Celebration Dinner for Non-Vegetarians

MURGH KA SOUP
Chicken Soup

KABAB KA KHORMA
Kabab Curry

PRAWN VINDALOO
Hot and Spicy Pork Curry

SALIM RAAN
*Roasted Spicy Whole
Leg of Lamb*

URAD KI SAABUT DAAL
Whole Black Bean Curry

PESHAWARI NAAN
*Enriched Leavened
Bread*

**PEELE ZEERE WALE
CHAWAL**
Yellow Rice

PARWAL BHAJI

**TAMATAR AUR LAHSUN
KI CHUTNEY**
*Tomato and Garlic
Chutney*

SIRKE 'WALE' PYAZ
Onion Rings in Vinegar

NIMBU KA ACHAAR
Lime Pickle

KULFI
Indian Ice Cream

NARIYAL KI BARFI
Coconut Fudge

TARBOOZ KI SHARBAT
Watermelon Sherbet

Serves twelve to fourteen people

MURGH KA SOUP
clear chicken soup

This is a clear, light soup—very delicately spiced, and is an ideal starter to any substantial meal.

YOU WILL NEED

2 tbsp butter

6 cloves

2 tsp crushed coriander seeds

4 bay leaves

3 oz (75 g) onion, sliced

116 oz (450 g) chicken pieces with bone

1 tsp salt, or to taste

large pinch freshly milled black pepper

3 pints (900 ml) water

1 tsp lemon juice, preferably freshly squeezed

FOR GARNISHING:

5-6 croutons per serving

In a pressure cooker, melt the butter and add cloves, crushed coriander seeds and bay leaves. After a few seconds, when the cloves begin to swell, add the sliced onions and saute lightly.

Add chicken pieces and fry for about 5 minutes. Now add salt, black pepper and water and bring to boil. Pressure cook at 15 lbs pressure for 10-15 minutes. Remove from heat and strain. Add lemon juice and check seasoning, adjusting it if necessary.

Serve hot, garnished with croutons.

Handy Hint
To make croutons, deep fry small cubes of bread until crisp and golden in colour. Remove and drain on kitchen paper.

KABAB KA KHORMA
kabab curry

These kababs are baked and are rather soft in texture while the sauce has a smooth rich flavour (due to the use of almonds and coconut milk).

You Will Need *(For Kababs)*

2 ¹/₄ lbs (1 kg) minced lamb (twice minced)

4 oz (100 g) grated onions

4 cloves garlic, finely chopped

2" (5 cm) ginger, finely chopped

4 green chillies, finely chopped

2 tbsp mint leaves, finely chopped

2 tbsp fresh coriander leaves, finely chopped

2 tbsp garam masala

2 tsp salt, or to taste

4 tsp mustard oil

2 tsp lemon juice

2 eggs, lightly beaten

For Khorma Sauce

14 oz (400 g) grated onions

(For Kababs)
In a large bowl, combine all the ingredients and mix well.

Put this mixture through an electric grinder/food processor and mix further to blend all ingredients. Leave to stand for 15-20 minutes.

Divide the mixture into 35-40 parts and shape them into small bullet shaped kababs.

Place the kababs on to a greased baking tray and cook them in a very hot oven for 15-20 minutes. Turn them once in between to brown them all over.

Remove from oven and keep aside to cool.

(For Khorma Sauce)
Grind together the ginger and garlic with a little water. Keep aside.

Mix almond powder into the coconut milk. Keep aside.

Grind together the spices i.e., cloves, green cardamoms, peppercorns, cinnamon and red chillies with 1 cup water. Keep aside.

In a large pan heat ghee and fry onions until golden brown in colour. Add ginger-garlic and fry further for a minute or so.

Contd. ....

2 oz (60 g) fresh ginger

8 cloves garlic

2 oz (60 g) almond powder

16 fl oz (425 ml) coconut milk

7 oz (200 g) ghee

(Spices)

12 cloves

6 green cardamoms

20 peppercorns

4 x 1" (4 x 2.5 cm) piece of cinnamon

8 small whole red chillies

4 silver leaves for decoration

Then .add ground spices, and on low heat, fry for another few seconds. Add salt to taste.

Slowly add the coconut milk and almond mixture and let it cook for a while—do not let it thicken.

Gently add the cooked kababs, and on low heat allow them to simmer until the sauce turns thick and creamy in a few minutes.

Serve hot, decorated with silver leaves.

Handy Hints
1. These kababs may be prepared in advance as they freeze well!. But it is advisable to prepare the sauce freshly for best results.

2. To improve the garnish, slivered almonds (with skins) can be scattered on top of the silver leaves.

PRAWN VINDALOO
hot and spicy pork curry

SPICES TO BE GROUND TOGETHER

10 small red chillies, or kashmiri chillies

8-10 cloves garlic

1" (2.5 cm) fresh ginger

2 tsp mustard seeds

2 tsp cumin seeds

4 oz (115 g) onions

1" (2.5 cm) cinnamon stick

3-4 cloves

a few curry leaves

2 tsp salt

5 fl oz (150 ml) vinegar

YOU WILL NEED

2 lbs (900 g) large shelled prawns

5 fl oz (150 ml) vegetable cooking oil

1/2 tsp fenugreek seeds

4-5 green chillies, sliced

1/2" (1.25 cm) fresh ginger, shredded fine

1 tsp turmeric powder

Vindaloo is one of the several types of curries made in India. A speciality of Goa, which lies in the south-west region, vindaloos are extremely popular all over Southern India. Vindaloos always contain vinegar and have a reputation for being very hot and sour.

Prepare the spices to be ground into a smooth paste-like mixture and keep aside.

Heat oil. Season with fenugreek seeds. When they begin to splutter, add green chillies and fry for a few seconds. Do not brown. Add the ground spice paste along with the turmeric powder and fry on medium heat until the oil starts to separate. Add prawns and curry leaves and mix well. Fry for a further 3-5 minutes, stirring frequently, till oil separates once again.

Add vinegar and salt, cover and cook on low heat till prawns are tender and oil floats on top. Ideally, no water should be added and cooking should be completed on very low heat.

Handy Hints

1. It is preferable to use 'Degi mirch' or Kashmiri mirch, (which has a rich red colour, and is slightly less pungent) instead of the small red chillies.
2. If no water is used for grinding the spices, they will keep for several days in the fridge.
3. If a slightly thinner gravy is required, one cup of hot water may be added along with the vinegar.
4. Can use lamb, chicken, fish as alternatives.
5. Tiger prawns which are large & succelent are ideal for this recipe.

SALIM RAAN
roasted spicy whole leg of lamb

YOU WILL NEED

3-4 lbs (1.35-1.8 kg) whole leg of lamb, all surface fat trimmed off

FOR THE MARINADE

2 tsp meat tenderizer or raw papaya

1 tbsp fresh ginger

1 tbsp garlic

4 oz (115 g) onions, peeled, sliced and fried

1 tbsp garam masala powder

2 tbsp poppy seeds, dry roasted and ground

2 tbsp almond powder

1 tbsp salt

3-4 green chillies, chopped

4 tbsp fresh green coriander leaves

1 tbsp fresh mint leaves

A very special dish indeed and an attractive centrepiece, Salim raan is a real treat. Although the recipe looks complicated, it is really not so and you can always be sure of rewarding results.

Lay the whole leg of lamb on a chopping board. Hold your knife with its flat surface parallel to the board. Starting 1" (2.5 cm) away from the top end, make a clean horizontal cut (as close to the underlying bone as is possible) right along the length of the leg to just 2" (5 cm) away from the lower end. This should form a deep pocket of flesh.

Turn the leg of lamb over and make a second cut exactly in the same way as above. You should now end up with 3 horizontal layers which are still joined at the ends.

Rub the meat tenderizer all over the surfaces and into the cuts. Leave for half an hour.

For the marinade, liquidize all the ingredients together to make a smooth mixture. Rub this mixture thoroughly into the cut surfaces and all over the leg of lamb. Transfer the joint to a roasting pan and cover with aluminium foil. Refrigerate overnight or at least for 4-5 hours.

Pre-heat the oven to a high setting and place the covered tray in the oven. Bake for 35-40 minutes, turning the leg of lamb over once. Reduce the oven temperature to low and continue cooking with occasional basting (with juices from the pan) for another hour until the juices run clear and the lamb is tender. Then increase the oven temperature to high,

Contd. ....

5 fl oz (150 ml) natural yoghurt

4 fl oz (120 ml) ghee

For Garnishing:

2 tbsp toasted almond halves

silver leaves

uncover the joint, and bake for 5-10 minutes in order to crisp and brown the surface.

When ready to serve, place the silver leaves over the surface and sprinkle generously with the toasted almonds.

Carve at the table.

Handy Hints
1. This dish can be prepared fully a day in advance and simply re-heated when required.
2. Any juices remaining in the roasting pan can be saved to be used later for enriching curries.

URAD KI SAABUT DAAL
whole black bean curry

YOU WILL NEED
FOR COOKING WHOLE BLACK BEANS

12 oz (340 g) whole black beans

4 oz (120 g) red kidney beans

1"ginger, peeled and chopped

1 tsp red chilli powder

2 tsp salt or to taste

3 pints water

5 fl oz (150 ml) natural yoghurt, beaten

INGREDIENTS FOR SEASONING

4 fl oz (240 ml) ghee

4 oz (120 g) onions, peeled and finely sliced

1" ginger, peeled and finely shredded

3-4 green chillies

8 oz (250 g) tomatoes, blanched and chopped

5 fl oz (150 ml) cream

2 tsp garam masala powder

few fresh green coriander leaves (optional)

Urad ki saabut daal, with its smooth velvety texture and subtle flavour, is ideally suited for inclusion in almost any menu—be it simple or sumptuous.

To cook the daal
Wash the black and red beans thoroughly. Soak in 1 ¹/₂ pints (900 ml) of hot water and leave to stand for at least 3-4 hours or even overnight. Add salt, red chilli powder and ginger and pressure cook at 15 lbs pressure for about half an hour. Remove from heat and roughly mash beans and add the beaten yoghurt. Keep aside.

To season the daal
Heat ghee and fry the onions until golden brown. Add ginger, chopped green chillies and stir for a few seconds. Then add the tomatoes and cook covered on low heat until the tomatoes are soft and mushy. Pour this seasoning over the hot mashed daal and return to low heat and cook for a further 5 minutes.

When ready to serve re-heat daal, add cream, mix well and cook gently for 2-3 minutes. Serve sprinkled with garam masala and fresh coriander leaves.

This is one of the few daals which is nearly always served with Indian breads rather than with rice.

Handy Hint
If cooked a day in advance, the consistency of the daal will thicken. Correct this by adding a little boiled water to it.

PESHAWARI NAAN
enriched leavened bread

YOU WILL NEED

2 lb (450 g) plain flour

1/2 easy blend dried yeast or 1 oz (30 g) fresh yeast

2 tsp sugar

pinch salt

4 fl oz (120 ml) melted ghee

4 fl oz (120 ml) (approximately) milk

4 fl oz (120 ml) natural yoghurt

2 tsp baking powder

4 eggs

12 oz (360 g) crumbled home-made cheese

4 oz (120 g) mixed nuts (cashewnuts, pistachios, almonds), finely chopped

4 oz (120 g) dried mixed fruits (glace cherries, sultanas, apricots)

2 oz (60 g) butter

Peshawari naan is a much richer version of the ordinary naan, as it is stuffed with a mixture of home-made cottage cheese, dry fruits and nuts.

Make dough as for naan (see page 46)

Divide into 14 to 16 balls & keep.

Mix paneer, dried fruits and nuts together and keep aside.

Take each ball of dough and stuff it with about a tablespoonful of the cheese mixture. Roll it out gently and cook as for naans. After removing each of the cooked naans from the oven/grill, brush it with a little butter and sprinkle a little more of the mixture on top. Return it to the oven/grill for a further few seconds till the cheese starts to melt. Serve hot.

Handy Hint

To make kheema naan (naan stuffed with minced lamb): Use the mince mixture prepared for samosas (see page 178) as stuffing and proceed as for Peshawari naans.

Peele Zeere Wale Chawal
yellow savoury rice

You Will Need

12 oz (340 g) Basmati rice or any good quality long grain rice

24 fl oz (720 ml) water

2 tbsp ghee, or vegetable cooking oil

2 tsp black cumin seeds

1 tsp turmeric powder

1 tsp salt

Adding a touch of colour to any rice dish makes it look more interesting. As yellow is considered to be auspicious by most Indians, it is the favourite colour choice. Saffron is reserved for special occasions, as it is rather expensive. For everyday use, turmeric is a satisfactory natural alternative for imparting colour to any dish.

Clean and wash the rice in several changes of water, rubbing the rice gently between the fingers until the water runs clear.

Drain and soak rice in the measured amount of water and leave it to stand fo 15-20 minutes. Drain the rice through a sieve and save the water for later use.

Now heat ghee/oil in a large saucepan, add the cumin seeds and when they splutter, remove pan from heat. Add the turmeric and immediately afterwards add the drained rice. Stir and fry gently for 2-3 minutes till all the grains are well coated with oil. Add salt and the reserved water.

Bring the rice to boil. Stir gently once. Cover with a tight-fitting lid, reduce heat to very low, and cook for 10-12 minutes. Remove from heat. Leave covered and undisturbed for a further 5 minutes. Serve hot.

Handy Hint
The turmeric may be omitted altogether if desired—without affecting the flavour of this dish. In this case you will simply have cumin flavoured (white) rice.

Parwal Bhaji

You Will Need

2 lbs (900 g) parwal, washed and dried

1/2 tsp turmeric powder

1/2 tsp chilli powder

1 tsp salt

1 tsp cumin seeds

2 green chillies, slit lengthwise

4 tbsp cooking oil

This vegetable dish which is really simplicity in itself to prepare makes a welcome change with its mild and pleasant flavour.

Slice parwals lengthwise into quarters. Heat oil and add cumin seeds. When they begin to splutter, lower heat and add turmeric and chilli powders, green chillies and salt. Stir for a few seconds and add sliced parwals. Cover and cook in their own juices on low heat until they are tender but still retain a little crunchiness. Do not overcook. Serve hot.

Handy Hint

For variation in taste and appearance add 1 tsp lime juice and sprinkle a little desiccated coconut before serving.

TAMATAR AUR LAHSUN KI CHUTNEY
tomato and garlic chutney

YOU WILL NEED

¹/₂ lb (225 g) tomatoes

1-2 green chillies chopped fine or to taste,

1 tsp garlic paste

1 level tsp salt, or to taste

1 tbsp sugar

8-10 tbsp water

4 tbsp vinegar

This tomato and garlic chutney has a sweet and sour taste and will easily keep for a week or so in the fridge.

Scald the tomatoes, remove skin, and chop into small pieces.

Set a heavy-based saucepan over medium heat and place the chopped tomatoes, green chillies and garlic paste along with the water and cook until soft and pulpy.

Add salt and sugar and cook for a few minutes until the mixture thickens and acquires a glazed appearance.

Remove from heat, add vinegar, mix thoroughly and store in an air-tight jar in the fridge.

SIRKE WALE PYAAZ
onion rings in vinegar

YOU WILL NEED

6 oz (170 g) onions, peeled and sliced into fine rings

$\frac{1}{2}$ tsp salt, or to taste

$\frac{1}{4}$ tsp chilli powder

pinch tomato colouring

2 tbsp white wine vinegar

This simple onion relish is generally served with grilled meats, but is also suitable served as part of a full meal, whether vegetarian or non-vegetarian.

Mix all the above ingredients and put them in a saucepan on medium heat. Bring to boil. Remove from heat immediately. Cover and leave to cool. Serve in a small bowl.

Handy Hints

1. If using a microwave, place all the ingredients in a bowl, cover and cook on full power for 1-2 minutes. Cool and serve.

2. Peeled (whole) button onions may be used instead of onion rings.

NIMBU KA ACHAAR
lime pickle

YOU WILL NEED

12 oz (350 g) lime

4 tbsp salt

6 oz (170 g) fresh ginger cut into slivers approximately $^1/_4$" (0.5 cm) thick

1 tsp chilli powder

pinch asafoetida (optional)

juice of 8 limes

Nimbu ka achaar is a lightly spiced pickle—tangy and sour. It also happens to be extremely popular partly because it is one of the simplest and most economical pickles to prepare.

Sterilize a glass or earthen screw-capped jar.

Wash and dry limes with a clean cloth. Cut the limes into quarters and rub them thoroughly with 2 tbsp salt. Place them in the prepared jar along with the ginger.

Strain the lime juice to remove any seeds and add the rest of the salt and chilli powder. Pour it over the limes in the jar and mix thoroughly. If using asafoetida, dry roast it first, before adding it to the lime juice. Screw on the cap tightly and keep the jar for 2-3 weeks in a warm and sunny place, remembering to shake it thoroughly everyday. The pickle should now be ready for use. Store in a cool and dry place and make sure the lid fits tightly.

Handy Hint
If desired, add 3 oz fresh whole green chillies (washed and thoroughly dried) along with the ginger.

KULFI
indian ice-cream

YOU WILL NEED

12 oz (340 g) evaporated milk, unsweetened

20 oz (560 g) sweetened condensed milk

20 fl oz (600 ml) thick double cream

2 tsp rose water

6-8 green cardamoms, shelled and seeds powdered

10 oz (300 g) blanched and chopped almonds and pistachio nuts, finely chopped

Kulfi, the original Indian ice-cream is an extremely rich dessert. There are various ways of making it, most of which require a great deal of time and effort. Kulfi made by the method shown below is virtually effortless, but nevertheless retains its true taste and appeal.

Kulfi is conventionally made in special conical aluminium moulds. If these are not available, use small yoghurt cartons with lids instead.

Take an extra large bowl and pour the double cream into it. Whisk the cream until slightly thickened but do not overwhisk. Add the evaporated and condensed milk and whisk again for 2-3 minutes. Then add the rose water, cardamom powder and chopped nuts.

Pour the mixture into moulds/cartons, tighten the lids and freeze upright for 4-5 hours.

The frozen kulfi will have a consistency suitable for cutting rather than scooping.

For best results, remember to transfer the kulfi moulds into the fridge (from the freezing compartment) for 15-20 minutes before serving.

At room temperature, kulfi melts fairly quickly as no binding agent such as gelatine is added to it.

Handy Hint
A simpler yet more attractive way to freeze kulfi is to pour the kulfi mixture into ice cube trays or any plastic container upto a depth of about 2" (5 cm). If using this method save a few nuts to scatter over the surface before freezing. If evaporated milk is not available reduce fresh full cream milk by boiling it down (with frequent stirring) to a third of its original quantity.

NARIYAL KI BARFI
coconut fudge

YOU WILL NEED

2 fresh coconut, finely grated or ground

12 fl oz (240 ml) water

12 oz (240 g) sugar

12 fl oz (360 ml) full cream milk

6 green cardamoms, shelled and seeds powdered

silver leaves to decorate

The coconut fruit which is grown in abundance in India finds many uses. It is tasty when eaten on its own, or can be dried to make curries and sweetmeats. The following recipe uses fresh coconuts which give by far the best results.

Grease a plate or dish with a very slightly raised edge and keep it aside.

Boil the water and sugar to make a thick syrup. To test if it is ready, put a drop of the syrup in a cup of water. If it settles to the bottom of the cup retaining its shape, the syrup is considered to be ready.

In a heavy saucepan, put the coconut and milk, and cook on medium heat stirring frequently until it is almost dry. Pour the prepared syrup over the coconut and keep stirring continuously to prevent it from sticking. Continue doing so until it is nearly but not completely dry.

Transfer the coconut mixture on the pre-greased plate/ dish and spread it out evenly.

Allow it to cool and then decorate with the silver leaves. Cut into diamond shaped pieces before serving.

Handy Hint
As barfi keeps well for a week or so, it can be prepared well in advance.

TARBOOZ KA SHARBAT
watermelon sherbet

YOU WILL NEED

2 lbs (840 g) water melon

6 fl oz (225 ml) water

2 tbsp castor sugar

pinch salt

6 oz (150 g) crushed ice cubes

large pinch dried ginger powder

Tarbooz ka sharbat is a cool, light and refreshing drink which looks as good as it tastes.

Remove the tough outer skin and deseed the watermelon. Scoop out 12-14 balls and save them for the garnish.

Place all the ingredients (except ginger powder and scooped out watermelon balls) in a liquidizer and liquidize for 2 minutes. Check seasoning and add more sugar if required.

Chill and serve in tall glasses garnished with watermelon balls. Sprinkle lightly with dry ginger powder.

Special Occasion Vegetarian Buffet

PANEER KHUBANI
Cottage Cheese and
Apricot Curry

BHARI HUI MIRCH
Capsicums Stuffed with
Lentils

SOOKHI KHUMBI
Indian Style Garlic
Mushrooms

CHANA TARI
Chick Pea Curry

NAVRATAN KHORMA
Mixed Vegetables in
a Rich, Creamy Sauce

**BAINGAN AKHROT KA
RAITA**
Yoghurt with Aubergines
and Walnuts

TIRANGA CHAWAL
Tri-coloured Rice

SHEERMAAL
Rich, Baked Bread

HARA SALAAD
Green Salad
(for details see page 74)

AVAKAI
Hot Green Mango Pickle

GULAB JAMUN
Milk Balls in Syrup

**LADDOO AUR AAM KI
KHEER**
Three-in-one Pudding

COFFEE
Essspresso Style
Indian Coffee
(for details see page 66)

SAUNF, ILAICHI
Aniseed and Green Cardamoms
(for details see page 66)

SUGGESTED DRINK
Fruit and Ginger Punch

Serves twelve to fourteen people

PANEER KHUBANI
cottage cheese and apricot curry

The unusual combination of dried apricots and home-made cheese gives this delightfully mild dish a slightly fruity taste.

YOU WILL NEED

6 oz (175 g) dried, stoned apricots

10 oz (310 g) cottage cheese/tofu

6 tbsp ghee

4 tbsp extra ghee, if using paneer

4 oz (115 g) onions, grated

1 tsp chilli powder

4 oz (115 g) tomatoes, blanched and chopped

2 oz (55 g) button onions

1 tsp salt, or to taste

10 fl oz (350 ml) water

$1/_2$ tsp saffron soaked in 1 tbsp milk

Soak the apricots in sufficient warm water to cover them for about an hour. Cut paneer/tofu into 1" cubes. If using tofu, wash it first in several changes of water. If using cottage cheese, shallow fry pieces until golden in colour and keep aside.

Heat ghee in a saucepan and fry the grated onions until brown. Add chilli powder and remove from heat immediately. Sprinkle a tablespoon of hot water and stir gently before returning the pan to heat. (This ensures that the chillies do not burn and gives a good colour.) Blend in the tomatoes and keep frying until ghee separates from the mixture.

Reduce heat to low and add the drained apricots, button onions and salt, and gently fry for 2-3 minutes. Add 8 fl oz (225 ml) hot water, cover and cook until the apricots are tender and only half the liquid remains. Gently mix in the fried paneer/tofu and saffron. Cover and cook for a further 4-5 minutes. (If the mixture appears to be dry, add the remaining 2 fl oz of hot water.) Serve hot.

Handy Hint
This dish can be enriched by the addition of 2-3 tbsp of double cream just before serving.

BHARI MIRCH
capsicums with a lentil stuffing

YOU WILL NEED

12-14 small sized green capsicums

vegetable cooking oil for shallow frying

thread for tying the capsicum 'lids'

FOR THE STUFFING

12 oz (340 g) split green gram (moong daal), without skin

oil

1 tsp cumin seeds

2 green chillies, deseeded and chopped fine

4 oz (110 g) finely chopped onions

1 tsp grated ginger

1 tsp salt, or to taste

1 tsp chilli powder

1 tsp turmeric powder

Capsicums may be filled with various ingredients, but this lentil filling is sure to be a winner, especially with vegetarians.

First prepare the stuffing. Wash and soak the daal for about 20 minutes in sufficient water to cover it completely. Drain off the water through a sieve and keep the daal aside.

In a heavy pan, heat the oil and add the cumin seeds. When they splutter, add the green chillies followed by the onions and ginger. Fry these for a minute or so but do not let them brown. Add salt, chilli and turmeric powders and after a few seconds put in the soaked and drained lentils. Stir gently for 2-3 minutes and then add the measured amount of water. Cover the pan with a tight-fitting lid, reduce heat and cook until the lentils are tender but not mushy. If some liquid remains uncover the pan and cook until the lentils are dry.

Remove from heat and stir in garam masala, lemon juice and chopped coriander leaves. Mix gently. Check seasoning and leave to cool.

Meanwhile, wash and dry the capsicums. Slice off the tops (save them for use as 'lids' later) and remove the seeds. Divide the lentil mixture into 4-6 parts (corresponding to the number of capsicums) and stuff each capsicum with the filling. Replace the capsicum 'lid' over the top and tie securely with the thread.

Set a heavy frying pan over medium heat. Heat sufficient oil to a depth of $^1/_4$" (0.5) cm for shallow frying and stand the capsicums upright in it. (Do not

Contd. ....

10 fl oz (300 ml) water
for cooking the moong daal

1 tsp garam masala
powder

2 tsp lemon juice

2 tbsp fresh green
coriander leaves, chopped

allow oil to get too hot or smoking—otherwise the capsicum skins will brown too quickly.) Cover and cook for 2-3 minutes and then turn the capsicums on their sides. Cover and cook further turning the capsicums over until they are slightly browned all around. This takes approximately 10 minutes. Remove the threads before serving.

Handy Hint

Instead of lentils, you can use a potato stuffing (see recipe for samosa filling page 178.)

SOOKHI KHUMBI
Indian style garlic mushrooms

YOU WILL NEED

1 lb (450 g) button mushrooms, washed and dried

2 tbsp butter

3 green chillies, finely chopped

4 cloves garlic, minced very fine

6 oz (170 g) spring onions, with stalks, chopped very fine

$1/2$ tsp freshly milled black pepper

1 tsp salt, or to taste

6 oz (170 g) fresh breadcrumbs

3 tsp lemon juice

vegetable oil for shallow frying

Mushrooms, a common sight in the Indian vegetable market in winter, are considered an extreme delicacy—associated almost always with special occasions. Here is our Indian version of the ever popular 'garlic mushrooms'.

Remove the stalks from the mushrooms to make a hollow cavity. Chop up the stalks finely.

Melt butter in a frying pan. Add the green chillies, minced garlic, spring onions and after a few seconds the mushroom stalks. Stir and fry for another minute and then add the freshly milled black pepper and salt. Remove from heat. Add fresh breadcrumbs and lemon juice. Mix thoroughly and allow to cool.

Fill the hollow mushrooms with this mixture.

Heat a little oil in a heavy frying pan (preferably non-stick) and put in the mushrooms no more than a single layer thick, filled side facing up. Turn heat to low, cover pan and gently saute, the mushrooms for 2-3 minutes. Turn them over carefully just once and cook covered for another minute or so.

Fill the hollow mushrooms tightly with this mixture otherwise the filling might spill out when mushrooms are turned over while frying.

Handy Hint

To turn these into garlic mushroom fritters, make a thick batter with cornflour and egg white, a large pinch of salt and pepper. Dip the stuffed mushrooms, coating them fully with the batter. Deep fry in hot oil until light brown. Drain on kitchen paper and serve with any chutney or sauce.

CHANA TARI
chick pea curry

YOU WILL NEED

11b (450 g) chick peas/
kabuli chana

2 tsp salt, or to taste

1 tsp turmeric powder

8 tbsp ghee

8 oz (230g) onions, peeled
and grated

1 tsp chilli powder

8 oz (230g) tomatoes,
peeled and chopped

2 tbsp garam masala

3 ½ pint (2 litre) water

Compared with many other curries, the gravy for this recipe is not too rich. It forms an ideal combination with any rice dish.

Wash the chick peas thoroughly and soak in water, preferably overnight. Cook the chick peas with salt, and turmeric powder in a pressure cooker for half an hour at 15 lbs pressure. Allow the pressure to drop by itself. They should be soft but not mushy.

In a saucepan, heat the ghee and fry onions till golden brown. Add chilli powder and stir for a few seconds, before adding the chopped tomatoes. Stir and fry on medium heat till tomatoes are well blended and ghee separates.

Pour the remaining liquid from the cooked chanas into the fried masala mixture and bring it to a boil.

Gently add the cooked chick peas. Cover and cook on low heat for a further 10 - 15 minutes.

If the mixture seems dry, add a little boiled water to get the required consistency. Sprinkle garam masala powder, stir and serve hot.

Handy Hint

Chick peas can be frozen and are an ideal item to have in the freezer.

NAVRATAN KHORMA
Mixed vegetables in a rich cream sauce

YOU WILL NEED

1 ¹/₂ lbs (675 g) prepared mixed vegetables such as carrots, french beans, sweet corn, mushrooms, peas

6 oz (170 g) onions, peeled and grated

2 green chillies, deseeded and finely chopped

2 tomatoes skinned and chopped

1 tsp salt, or to taste

4 tbsp natural yoghurt, lightly beaten

10 fl oz (300 ml) hot water

FOR GARNISHING:

1 tbsp fresh coriander leaves, finely chopped

Spices to be ground separately into a paste with the help of a little water:

1" (2.5 cm) fresh ginger, scraped

3 cloves of garlic

1 tbsp poppy seeds, dry roasted

2 tbsp grated coconut

The imaginative use of different ingredients results in an astounding variety of sauces/gravies which are a hallmark of Indian cuisine. Thick, rich sauces/gravies are produced by the addition of ingredients such as natural yoghurt, onions, tomatoes, coconut, poppy seeds, ground almonds etc. In the following vegetable khorma recipe, we have used poppy seeds and coconut not only to thicken the sauce but also to enrich the flavour.

Heat oil in a heavy pan, add the spices for seasoning i.e., cinnamon, cloves, and green cardamoms. Fry for a few seconds then add grated onions and continue frying until onions are golden brown. Now add the green chillies and ginger-garlic paste, stir and fry for a minute or so until the raw garlic smell disappears. Take care not to brown the ginger-garlic.

Add carrots and beans and fry for 2-3 minutes followed by sweet corn, peas, and mushrooms. Fry all the vegetables for a further 2-3 minutes on low heat. Add chopped tomatoes, stir and fry again for a minute or two, adding a sprinkling of hot water now and then to prevent the mixture from sticking to the pan. When the vegetables are half cooked add the beaten yoghurt, poppy seed and coconut pastes. Keep stirring and frying until all the moisture disappears and oil begins to separate.

Pour in the hot water, cover and cook on low heat for a further 5 minutes. If the sauce/gravy appears too thick, adjust by adding a little more hot water and letting the khorma simmer for a little while longer.

Serve hot, garnished with coriander leaves.

Handy Hint

To vary the taste, add a few sultanas and cashewnuts along with the vegetables.

BAINGAN AKHROT KA RAITA
yoghurt with aubergines and walnuts

YOU WILL NEED

2 medium sized aubergine, roasted

15 fl oz (570 ml) natural yoghurt

1 tsp salt, or to taste

1 tsp freshly ground pepper

3 tbsp chopped walnuts (save a little for garnish)

3 tbsp finely chopped celery (save a little for garnish)

This long forgotten recipe uses the somewhat unusual combination of aubergines and walnuts to good effect.

Roast the aubergines under a hot grill or over a gas flame, until the skin gets a charred look and the vegetable is soft to touch. Skin the aubergine and mash the pulp lightly with a fork.

Put the yoghurt into a serving bowl and whisk it along with the salt and pepper until it is smooth and creamy.

Add the mashed aubergine, chopped walnut and celery. Mix lightly. Sprinkle the reserved celery and walnut on top and serve chilled.

Handy Hints

1. Try not to leave the peeled and mashed aubergine on its own for too long as it tends to discolour. Add it to the yoghurt as soon as possible.

2. To give this raita a more festive look: stand a stick of celery with a few young leaves in the centre of the bowl and pour the yoghurt mixture around it. Decorate with walnut halves as desired.

Tiranga Chawal
tri-coloured rice

You Will Need

12 oz (340 g) Basmati rice

24 fl oz (720 ml) water

3 tbsp ghee or vegetable cooking oil

4-5 cloves

6-8 peppercorns

3-4 green cardamoms

1" piece (2.5 cm) cinnamon

2-3 bay leaves

1 tsp salt

1/4 tsp yellow food colour mixed with 1 tsp water

1/4 tsp red food colour mixed with 1 tsp water

Tiranga chawal gives the impression that much skill and hard work will be necessary in the preparation of this dish. In fact, it requires the least amount of effort.

Clean and wash the rice in several changes of water, running your finger through the rice until the water runs clear.

Drain and soak rice in the measured amount of water and leave it to stand for 15-20 minutes. Then drain the rice through a sieve and reserve the water for later use.

In a large heavy-based pan, heat ghee or oil and add the whole spices. Stir and fry for a few seconds till they begin to splutter. Add the drained rice and salt and fry gently for 2-3 minutes until all the grains are well coated with ghee/oil. Add the reserved water, turn heat up to high and bring to a boil.

Stir the rice gently once, cover with a tight-fitting lid, reduce heat to low and cook for 10 to 12 minutes. Remove pan from heat and leave undisturbed for a further 5 minutes.

Then remove lid, and with the help of a long skewer make about 6 deep holes in the rice. Pour a little of the colouring in each hole. It is best to alternate the colours. Now mix the entire contents of the pan gently with a wooden spatula—this ensures that quite a few grains of rice get coloured. Serve hot.

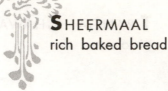

SHEERMAAL
rich baked bread

The ingredients for sheermaal are more or less the same as for naan, but its mode of preparation helps it to retain its moist and soft texture for a longer period.

YOU WILL NEED

15 fl oz (450 ml) milk

2 eggs, beaten lightly

10 fl oz (300 ml) cooking oil/ghee

2 tsp rose water

1½ lb (675 g) plain flour

2 tsp baking powder

2 tbsp castor sugar

1 tsp salt

½ oz (12 g) dried yeast granules or 1 oz (30 g) fresh yeast

6 green cardamoms, shelled and powdered

FOR BRUSHING OVER

2 oz (55 g) butter

2½ fl oz (75 ml) milk

Warm the milk slightly (to tepid) and add the lightly beaten egg, cooking oil/ghee, and rose water and keep aside.

Sift together the flour, baking powder, castor sugar, salt, easy blend dry yeast, and powdered cardamoms. Make a smooth, soft and pliable dough with the help of the milk mixture using only as much of it as necessary. Knead vigorously for a few minutes. Cover and leave in a warm place for about half an hour. Do not stand the dough for much longer.

Pre-heat the oven to its highest setting and place the baking tray inside to keep it hot and ready for use.

Divide the dough into 16-20 equal portions. Make them into round balls, and with the help of a little dry flour, roll them into thick pancakes 6-8" (15-20 cm) across.

Prick them with a fork in three or four places to prevent them from puffing up. Lay them in batches of 3 or 4 on the baking tray and bake for just under 5 minutes—until light golden in appearance with a few brown spots just showing. (Do not overcook as this will make the bread hard.) There is no need to turn the sheermaal.

Remove sheermaal from the baking tray with the help of a wooden spatula, and with the milk. Coat only one side with melted ghee as well. Allow the

136

Contd. ....

sheermaal to cool before stacking them together, or else they will stick to each other.

Interleave 3-4 sheermaals with layers of grease-proof paper and wrap in kitchen foil. These can easily be stored in the fridge for 4-5 days.

To warm them up before serving, place with foil for 5 minutes or so in a hot oven or remove foil and heat in a microwave for 1 minute only at medium power.

Handy Hints

1. If entertaining a strict vegetarian, use natural yoghurt (equal in weight to the egg) instead of the egg.

2. If using a food processor, first make the milk mixture together with the egg and oil and then add the remaining ingredients into the bowl and process to form a dough.

Avakai
hot green mango pickle

You Will Need

2 lbs (900 g) very firm raw green mangoes, preferably of the small variety

4 oz (300 g) salt

2 tbsp turmeric powder

4 oz (115 g) red chilli powder—more if required

25 fl oz (750 ml) gingelly oil

1 tbsp fenugreek seeds

handful of curry leaves

3 whole pods of garlic, peeled and cloves kept whole

4 oz (115 g) mustard seeds, freshly powdered

2 tsp asafoetida

Every grandmother in India seems to have her own favourite green mango pickle recipe. This fiery and long lasting pickle is typically South Indian in style.

Special Requirements

A large saucepan (preferably not aluminium): sterilized earthenware or glass jar with a tight-fitting lid.

Wash and wipe dry the mangoes thoroughly. Cut them into fours, or into 1-1 $\frac{1}{2}$" (3-4 cm) pieces. Mix together the salt, turmeric and red chilli powders. Rub them well into the mango pieces and keep aside.

Heat oil in a large pan set on medium heat. Add fenugreek seeds and curry leaves. When they start to splutter add the whole cloves of garlic and stir for a few seconds. Do not brown. Add mustard powder and asafoetida. Stir for a minute or so. Remove the pan from heat and add the mango pieces. Mix thoroughly. Cover and leave it to cool.

Transfer the contents of the pan to a sterilized jar ensuring that the mango pieces are completely immersed in oil. If needed, heat a little more oil and add to the mangoes.

This pickle will take 2-3 weeks to mature i.e., to be ready to use. Do remember to keep it in a warm place, preferably in the sun, and shake the jar everyday during that period.

GULAB JAMUN
milk balls in syrup

YOU WILL NEED

FOR THE SYRUP

30 fl oz (900 ml) water

1lb (450 g) sugar

4 green cardamoms, shelled and seeds powdered

few strands of saffron

1 tbsp rose essence

FOR THE GULAB JAMUNS

4 oz (110 g) self raising flour or 4 oz (100 g) plain flour and large pinch baking powder

2 tsp semolina

1lb (450 g) full cream milk powder

4 green cardamoms

2 oz (60 g) butter

2 pint (1200 ml) full cream milk made into paneer and crumbled (see method page 7)

Most Indians have a very sweet tooth and therefore gulab jamuns, sweet as they are, tend to be a great favourite. These are delicious, served hot or cold.

For making the syrup
Set a large pan on medium heat. Prepare the syrup by boiling together the water, sugar, crushed cardamom seeds and saffron, until three fourths of the original quantity of water remains. Cool the syrup and add the rose essence.

For the gulab jamuns
Sieve together the flour, semolina, milk powder and the powdered cardamoms. Rub in the melted butter and crumbled paneer. Make a soft pliable dough with the help of slightly warmed milk. Cover and leave it to rest for at least half an hour. Divide into 24 pieces and shape into round balls.

Heat the ghee along with the cooking oil in a deep frying pan or kadhai on low heat and fry a few of the gulab jamun balls at a time (do not overcrowd the pan). They should be fried slowly on low heat until golden brown all over. This is important in order to ensure that they cook thoroughly from the inside. Therefore, be careful that the ghee/oil does not get too hot.

Remove the gulab jamuns and keep aside. Finish frying all the gulab jamuns in this way. Gently drop them into the syrup and place the pan over low heat. Cover the pan with a tight-fitting lid and heat gently for 10 minutes. Do not uncover the pan but leave it in a warm place for a few hours or overnight for the

Contd. ....

10 fl oz (300 ml)
(approximately) milk

16 fl oz (450 ml) ghee

16 fl oz (450 ml)
vegetable cooking oil

syrup to soak into the gulab jamuns.

Gulab jamuns can be served hot or cold. To serve hot, re-heat along with the syrup for a few minutes on medium heat.

Handy Hints

1. Gulab jamuns warm up within seconds in a microwave.

2. Gulab jamuns can also be served with thick double cream.

LADDOO AUR AAM WALI KHEER
Laddoos & mango rice pudding

You Will Need

1 ³/₄ lbs (800 g) rice pudding, tinned or freshly made.

1 lb 2 oz (500 g) mango pulp

2 fresh mangoes or tinned mangoes

14 oz (400 g) laddoos (broken)

¹/₂ pint (300 ml) double cream

2 tsp rose water

few strands of saffron

few chopped pistachios

Here is a quick baked pudding. The variety of ingredients marry well and produce an highly aromatic flavour.

Mix together the rice pudding, (method given on page 22) mango pulp, cream and rose water in a baking dish.

Cover with mango slices and sprinkle laddoo mixture all over. Also scatter the saffron strands.

Bake covered in a hot oven for half an hour.

Sprinkle pistachios and bake uncovered for a further 10 minutes until golden brown. Serve hot.

Handy Hints
1. Dermerara sugar may be used as an alternative to laddoos.

2. This pudding may be baked in the microwave (approximately 6 minutes followed by a further 2 minutes).

FRUIT AND GINGER PUNCH

You Will Need

1 pint (600 ml) water

10 oz (275 g) sugar

1 pints (600 ml) orange juice

4 lemons, juice extracted

4 tsp juice of fresh root ginger

4 oz (110 g) tinned pineapple, finely chopped

1 pint (600 ml) soda water

Ginger occupies a unique place in Indian cookery. The use of ginger juice in this fruit punch gives it an unusual flavour.

Put the water and sugar into a pan, bring to a boil and let it continue to simmer in order to prepare a thick syrup of 3 thread consistency. Remove from heat and cool thoroughly. Add the juices of orange, lemon and ginger along with the pineapple pieces and chill thoroughly.

When ready to serve, add the chilled soda water and serve at once.

Special Occasion Non-Vegetarian Buffet

KADHAI CHICKEN SPECIAL
Pan-fried Chicken

HARE PYAZ WALE JHINGE
King Prawns with Spring Onions

TALI MACHLI
Deep Fried Fish

SOOKHE KABULI CHANE
Dry Spicy Chick Peas

ALOO TUK
Spiced Deep Fried Potatoes

HYDERABADI BIRYANI
Classic, Rich Rice Dish with Lamb

BHATURE
Deep Fried Leavened Bread

DAHI CHUTNEY
Seasoned Yoghurt

HARA SALAAD
Green Salad
(For details see page 74)

GAJAR KA ACHAAR
Carrot Pickle

MALAIPURA
Indian Cream Pancakes

AAM AUR LYCHEE KA MITHA
Mango and Lychee Dessert

COFFEE
Esspresspo Style 'Indian' Coffee

MISHRI AUR SAUNF
Crystallized Sugar and Aniseed

VERANDAH PUNCH
A Cool and Refreshing Drink

Serves twelve to fourteen people

KADHAI CHICKEN
pan fried chicken

Only the best chicken pieces are used for this exquisite, medium-dry dish which is eminently suitable for any special occasion.

YOU WILL NEED

FOR THE MARINADE

3 lbs (1.35 kg) boneless breast of chicken

3 tbsp natural yoghurt

2" piece (5 cm) fresh root ginger

6 fat cloves of garlic

1 tsp chilli powder

$\frac{1}{2}$ tsp turmeric powder

2 tsp salt

INGREDIENTS FOR MASALA MIXTURE

5 fl oz (150 ml) vegetable cooking oil

6 oz (170 g) onions, finely sliced

8 oz (225 g) onions, ground

1 $\frac{1}{2}$ tsp cumin powder

2 tsp coriander powder

2 tbsp poppy seeds, dry roasted and ground

2-4 green chillies, deseeded, finely chopped

2 tbsp fresh coriander leaves, finely chopped

1 tbsp fresh mint leaves finely chopped

8 oz (225 g) tomatoes, chopped and peeled

6 fl oz (150 ml) natural yoghurt

1 tbsp lemon juice

Heavy based kadhai

Skin the chicken breast and cut into approximately 3" x 1" (7.5 cm) pieces. Grind all spices for the marinade to a smooth mixture. Apply to the chicken pieces and keep aside for two to three hours.

Heat oil in a kadhai and fry sliced onions till golden brown. Remove these from oil and keep aside. Reheat the same oil and now fry the ground onions till light pink in colour. Add cumin, coriander and poppy seed powders. Fry gently till oil begins to separate from the mixture. Add green chillies, coriander and mint leaves followed by the marinaded chicken to the above mixture and fry for a further 5 minutes, stirring frequently. Blend in the chopped tomatoes and yoghurt and continue frying for two to three minutes. Now add the previously fried onions and mix thoroughly. Cover and cook on low heat till chicken is tender. Sprinkle lemon juice and serve hot, ideally in a presentable looking kadhai. (explained on page12)

Handy Hints

1. The sliced fried onions may be used as a garnish instead of being incorporated into the dish.

2. Use lamb instead of chicken, but marinate it overnight, using twice the amount of yoghurt shown in the recipe.

HARE PYAZ WALE JHINGE
prawns with spring onions

YOU WILL NEED

8 tbsp vegetable cooking oil

1 tsp black cumin seeds

4 cloves

4 green cardamoms

6 oz (125 g) onions, finely chopped

1 tsp turmeric powder

1 tsp chilli powder

4 tbsp butter

10 oz (300 g) spring onions, with stalks chopped roughly

1 tsp garam masala powder

4 tsp lemon juice

2 lb (900 g) large prawns, shelled, and defrosted, if frozen

1 tsp salt or to taste

In the West, fresh prawns are a luxury; but in India, prawns of all kinds are found in plenty all along the coastal regions. The use of green spring onions in this recipe not only complements the flavour of the prawns but also gives it a distinguished appearance. For prawn lovers all over the world, this is a novel dish.

Heat the vegetable oil in a large, heavy-based frying pan. Add the black cumin seeds, cloves and green cardamoms, and fry for a few seconds till they swell. Immediately add the finely chopped onions and saute till pink. Stir in the turmeric and chilli powders and fry for a minute or so. Remove onions together with the whole spices and keep aside.

In the same pan, along with the remaining oil, melt butter, and fry prawns for 3-4 minutes on a high flame, stirring constantly.

Add chopped spring onions, and the previously fried onion mixture. Cook for 2-3 minutes. (If starting with raw prawns initially, a couple of extra minutes might be required for the prawns to just cook through.) Do not overcook. Remove from fire.

Sprinkle garam masala powder and lemon juice. Mix lightly, and serve hot.

Handy Hints

1. Select the largest prawns possible as they are more succulent.

2. In order to stretch this dish a little further, increase the quantity of either onions or spring onions.

TALI HUI MACHLI
fried fish

YOU WILL NEED

12-14 thick cod steaks or any firm fleshed white fish approximately 1" (2.5 cm) thick

2 tsp salt

2 tsp turmeric powder

3 tsp garam masala powder

2 tsp chilli powder

3 tbsp lemon juice, or more to taste

vegetable oil for deep frying

'Fried fish' invariably means fish fried in batter in the West, but in India, fish is generally fried without using any batter. The following recipe, simple as it is, produces excellent results.

Wash and dry the fish thoroughly. Sprinkle salt, turmeric, garam masala and chilli powders along with the lemon juice on the fish and set it aside for at least half an hour.

Heat the oil to near smoking point. Reduce heat and deep fry the fish pieces a few at a time, until golden brown on both sides, turning them over once. Drain on kitchen paper and serve hot.

Handy Hints
To vary the flavour, 2 tsp. each of ginger and garlic paste may also be added to the fish along with the rest of the ingredients.

SOOKHE KABULI CHANE
dry spicy chick peas

Kabuli chane make a hearty, satisfying dish which also happens to be protein-rich. It is immensely popular, particularly with vegetarians, and is an appropriate choice for a special meal. However, it is equally good served on its own as a snack.

YOU WILL NEED

11b (450 g) chick peas (kabuli chane)

3 $\frac{1}{2}$ pints (2 litre) water

2 tsp salt

1 tsp chilli powder

6 oz (150 g) ghee

4 oz (100 g) finely shredded ginger

6 green chillies, finely sliced

2 tbsp cumin seeds, roasted and powdered

2 tbsp dried mango powder

$\frac{1}{2}$ tsp red food colouring (optional)

4 oz (100 g) onions, finely sliced

2 tsp garam masala

FOR GARNISHING:

few green coriander leaves and
lemon wedges

Wash the chick peas thoroughly and soak them in water, preferably overnight. Cook the chick peas with salt, and chilli powder (using the water in which they were soaked) in a pressure cooker for half an hour at 15 lbs pressure. Allow the pressure to drop by itself. The chick peas should be soft but not mushy.

In a frying pan, heat ghee and fry the ginger and green chillies till light brown. Remove from heat and add cumin seeds, mango powder and food colouring (optional). Stir well and pour the mixture over the cooked chick peas. Return to heat. Add raw sliced onions and cook further for 10 to 15 minutes on low heat, or till all the juices are absorbed.

Remove from heat and sprinkle garam masala powder and coriander leaves. If the mixture seems a little too dry add an extra tablespoon of ghee.

Serve decorated with lemon wedges.

Handy Hints

1. If desired, add 6 oz (150 g) boiled cubed potatoes along with cumin seeds and mango powder.

2. Kabuli chane freeze very successfully; but do not add potatoes if freezing them.

ALOO TUK
spiced deep fried potatoes

YOU WILL NEED

vegetable oil for deep frying

2 lb (900 g) medium sized, preferably new potatoes

2 tsp garam masala powder

2 tsp salt

1 tsp red chilli powder

2 tsp dry mango powder

2 tsp dry roasted cumin seed powder

1 tsp rock salt or sea salt

1 tsp freshly milled black pepper

These are crisp, spicy, deep fried potatoes with a difference!

Wash, peel and dry the potatoes. Cut them lengthwise into two.

Heat the oil in a deep pan and fry the potato halves, a few at a time, on medium heat until golden brown. Drain and leave to cool. Sprinkle salt over them and leave for a while.

Meanwhile, mix the rest of the ingredients in a small bowl and keep aside, ready for later use. Flatten each fried potato half by pressing it firmly between your palms, taking care not to let it disintegrate.

Re-heat the oil and fry the flattened potato halves in batches until they turn brown and their edges turn crisp. Remove and drain. Arrange in a single layer on a serving platter. Sprinkle the mixed spice powder generously all over and serve immediately.

Handy Hint
These double fried potatoes may be left to keep warm in a hot oven to retain their crispness and the spices sprinkled over them just before serving.

HYDERABADI BIRYANI
classic, rich rice dish with lamb

Biryanis are the finest and richest of all rice preparations and, therefore, are served only on special occasions. This particular simplified recipe comes from Hyderabad, which lies in the Southern part of India and is well-known for its cuisine within the country. Cooking biryani to perfection is an art in itself, one which requires some skill and judgment. Hyderabadi biryani is almost a meal in itself, but when served with other items, it is undoubtedly the centre of attention at the table.

YOU WILL NEED

FOR THE MARINADE

3 lbs (1kg. 400 g) leg of lamb, cut into 2" (5 cm) pieces

2 tsp raw papaya (ground), or $1\frac{1}{2}$ tsp meat tenderizer

12 oz (350 g) ghee

16 oz (450 g) onions, finely sliced

20 fl oz (550 ml) natural yoghurt

4 tbsp lemon juice, freshly squeezed

10 cloves garlic, peeled

3" (7.5 cm) root ginger, peeled

8 green chillies

4 tbsp chopped green coriander leaves

2 tbsp fresh mint leaves, chopped or 1 tbsp dried mint

For marinading
Wash and dry the lamb pieces and rub in the ground raw papaya or meat tenderizer. Keep aside.

Heat ghee and deep fry the sliced onions until golden brown. Remove and keep aside. (Also reserve some for garnish later.)

Liquidize together the natural yoghurt, lemon juice, ginger, garlic, green chillies, fresh mint and coriander leaves and salt so that a smooth mixture is formed. Pour this mixture over the lamb pieces and add the fried onions as well. Mix well and set aside for 8 - 12 hours or preferably overnight in the fridge.

To part-cook the rice
Wash the rice in several changes of water and drain. In a large pan, place the rice, water, salt and oil. Bring to a boil and cook for a few minutes. Watch it very carefully as the rice needs to be only half cooked. To test this, take a grain of rice and press it between the thumb and forefinger—you should be able to feel a hard inner core. (It is important not to let the rice cook fully.) Immediately, drain the rice and run cold water over it. This is to prevent the rice from

Contd. ....

2 tsp salt, or to taste

3 tbsp almond powder

FOR THE RICE

2 lb (900 g) Basmati rice

8 pints (4.50 litres) water

2 tbsp salt

3 tbsp ghee or cooking oil

FOR ASSEMBLING THE BIRYANI

4 x1" (2.5 cm) cinnamon stick

6 whole green cardamoms

a few strands of saffron soaked in 2 $\frac{1}{2}$ fl oz (75 ml) warm milk

FOR GARNISHING

1 tsp red food colour (optional)

1 tsp yellow food colour (optional)

A few crisply fried onion rings

cooking further in its own steam. Drain and keep it aside.

To assemble and cook the biryani
Re-heat the same ghee in which the onions were fried. Add cinnamon and cardamoms and fry for a few seconds.

Pour the entire contents of the marinated lamb over the hot ghee. Do not stir. Cover the pan immediately and cook on low heat for 20-30 minutes.

Then uncover pan, and put in the half cooked rice over the lamb and spread it evenly. Do not mix or stir. Quickly pour the milk and saffron mixture all over the rice and immediately cover with a tight-fitting lid. Increase the heat to high and cook for a few minutes until steam begins to form.

Now turn down the heat to very low and cook further for at least half an hour. Do not open the lid once the steam is formed or else steam will escape and the biryani will not cook properly. (If the lid is not tight-fitting and steam is escaping, cover pan with a double layer of aluminium foil, replace the lid and put something really heavy on it.)

When the cooking time is over, remove the pan from heat and leave it undisturbed for the next 20 minutes.

To serve the biryani
Uncover the pan and sprinkle the two food colourings (if using) all over the rice. With a wooden spatula, gently but thoroughly mix the entire contents of the pan.

Dish out the biryani on a large rice platter and scatter the reserved fried onions.

Handy Hints
1. As this is a time consuming item to prepare, it may be fully cooked a day in advance and thoroughly

Contd. ....

re-heated before serving—either in a microwave or in a hot oven.

2. The food colouring only adds to the appearance and can be omitted entirely if wished as it makes no difference to the taste or flavour.

3. Remember to check that the lamb must be of good quality, otherwise it might need a little more cooking, before adding rice.

4. Chicken instead of lamb is a very popular and welcome change.

BHATURA
deep fried bread

Bhaturas are a favourite leavened, deep fried bread, which form a classic combination with kabuli chane, but are also relished with a variety of other dishes.

YOU WILL NEED

11b (450 g) plain flour

pinch salt

1 tsp sodium bicarbonate

6 fl oz (150 ml) natural yoghurt, beaten

2 whole egg, lightly beaten (optional)

2 tsp sugar

3 tsp ghee

a little warm water if needed

oil for deep frying

Sieve the flour, salt, and sodium bicarbonate into a large bowl. Warm the yoghurt slightly and add it along with the beaten egg, and sugar into the flour to form a soft, but not sticky dough.

Continue kneading, adding the ghee as you go along, till the dough is smooth and elastic. Cover it with a damp cloth and leave it in a warm place for 2 to 3 hours, till it is well risen.

Divide into 20-24 equal parts, shape into balls, and roll out with the help of a little dry flour into rounds of 4" (10 cm) diameter, and $1/8$" (3 mm) thickness. Keep them covered. Heat oil on medium heat and deep fry each round, turning once till puffed up and both sides are golden brown. Remove, drain on a paper towel and serve hot.

Handy Hints

1. To vary the flavour, add 1-2 tbsp crushed dried fenugreek leaves to the flour.

2. Add 2 tsp cumin seeds to the flour for a different flavour.

DAHI CHUTNEY
seasoned yoghurt

YOU WILL NEED

10 fl oz (300 ml) natural yoghurt

2 tbsp desiccated coconut or 2 tbsp freshly grated coconut

2 tbsp finely chopped onion

2 green chilli, deseeded and finely chopped

1 tsp salt, or to taste

FOR THE SEASONING

2 tbsp cooking oil

1 tsp mustard seeds, small variety

8-10 curry leaves

4 whole red chillies

There are very few chutneys which are specifically served with a particular dish, but dahi chutney invariably accompanies biryanis.

Beat the yoghurt well and add the coconut, onion, salt and green chillies. Mix well and keep aside in a serving dish.

To season the dahi
In a small pan, heat the cooking oil to near smoking point, add the mustard seeds, curry leaves and the whole red chillies. As soon as the seeds start to splutter, remove the pan from heat and pour its entire contents over the beaten yoghurt mixture. Cover the dish immediately in order to allow the flavours to infuse.

HARA SALAAD
Green salad

(For details see page 74)

Gajar Ka Achaar
carrot pickle

You Will Need

8 oz (225 g) carrots

2 tbsp cooking oil

pinch asafoetida

1 oz (25 g) chilli powder

1 oz (25 g) mustard, coarsely powdered

1 oz (25 g) salt or more if required

1 tsp turmeric powder

4 fl oz (120 ml) lemon juice

The glut of seasonal carrots and the ready use of spices have resulted in this simple pickle from the Western region of India. The pickle is quite easy to prepare and is a happy blend of contrasting flavours. It will keep easily for a few months in an air-tight jar.

Wash the carrots thoroughly and cut into 2"x $\frac{1}{2}$" (5 cm x 1.25 cm) long pieces. Dry with a clean cloth.

Heat the oil and fry the asafoetida for a few seconds. Remove the pan from heat and add all the ingredients except lemon juice. Mix thoroughly and cool. Then add the lemon juice and mix again. Store in a sterilized glass jar.

Serve a few tablespoons with the meal.

Handy Hint

To make carrot and chilli pickle: slit green chillies lengthwise, and fill cavity with a mixture of salt and turmeric powder. Add these to the carrot pickle as given above.

MALAIPURA
indian cream pancakes

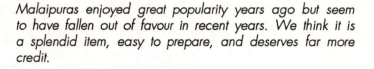

Malaipuras enjoyed great popularity years ago but seem to have fallen out of favour in recent years. We think it is a splendid item, easy to prepare, and deserves far more credit.

YOU WILL NEED

FOR THE PANCAKES

10 oz (200 g) plain flour

6 fl oz (180 ml) double cream, enough to form a pouring batter

cooking oil for shallow frying

FOR THE SYRUP

8 oz (230 g) sugar

12 fl oz (360 ml) water

4 green cardamoms, shelled and seeds crushed

2 tsp rose water

a few strands of saffron

FOR GARNISHING

2 tbsp coarsely chopped pistachios

2 tbsp blanched almonds

4 tbsp extra thick cream

Mix together the plain flour and cream to get a batter of thick pouring consistency i.e., similar to pancake batter. Leave it to rest for half an hour and mix well again.

Set a heavy-based frying pan on medium heat and add enough cooking oil to coat the base of the pan. Place a small ladleful of the batter and shallow fry the malaipura on both sides, turning it over once, until golden brown.

Remove, drain and keep aside. Repeat until all the batter is used up.

To make the syrup
Place the sugar in water in a saucepan along with the crushed cardamom seeds and bring to boil. Keep cooking until the syrup thickens. Remove from the fire, and when cool, add rose water, saffron strands and keep aside.

To assemble
When ready to serve, arrange the puras (pancakes) in a single layer on an oven-proof platter.

Top each pura with 1-2 tsp of the prepared syrup. Scatter the chopped nuts over it (the more the better) and place the dish in a very hot oven for 2-3 minutes. Serve hot.

Contd. ....

Handy Hints

1. To vary the flavour, omit the cardamom and rose water from the syrup, but instead add 1 tsp crushed aniseed when preparing the syrup.

2. Use yellow food colouring if not using saffron—though this will only provide the colour, not the flavour of saffron.

3. Both puras (pancakes) and the syrup may be prepared a day in advance, leaving the final assembly for the last minute, just before serving.

COFFEE
esspresso style Indian coffee

(For details see page 66)

MISHRI AUR SAUNF
crystallized sugar and aniseed

The traditional way to end an Indian meal is to offer saunf with a sprinkling of mishri bits in it to the guests who help themselves to a large pinch of it. This does not involve any preparation at all.

AAM AUR LYCHEE KA MITHA
mango and lychee dessert

YOU WILL NEED

1¹/₂ lb (675 g) mango pulp, fresh or tinned

24 lychees, fresh or tinned

4 tbsp castor sugar, or more to taste

1 tsp saffron strands dissolved in 1 tbsp warm milk

10 fl oz (550 ml) double cream

Mangoes are known as the 'king of fruits' in India and have acquired a universal appeal. The arrival of the mango season is eagerly awaited by one and all and few can resist eating a ripe, juicy mango.

Mangoes form the basis of many a dessert and despite their distinct flavour, combine happily with other fruits. The following dessert requires very little time and effort to prepare.

Whip the cream lightly with the castor sugar. Fold in the mango pulp with the saffron. Mix well, check sweetness and add more sugar if desired. Add the stoned lychees, chill lightly and serve.

Handy Hint

If you wish to give this dessert a firmer texture, add a sachet of gelatine dissolved in hot water to the mango pulp. Mix this with the cream and allow it to set for 2-3 hours in the fridge before serving.

VERANDAH PUNCH
a cool and refreshing drink

YOU WILL NEED

juice of 2 large orange

juice of 2 thin skinned lemon

200 g sugar

6 fl oz (150 ml) water

10 fl oz (300 ml) freshly made tea, chilled

16 fl oz (450 ml) ginger ale, well chilled

16 fl oz (450 ml) soda water, well chilled

a few ice cubes

Thin slices of one large orange for garnishing

This is a cool and refreshing drink.

Mix together the fruit juices, sugar, water, and tea. Cool and strain into a bowl and chill. Just before serving mix in the ginger ale and soda water. Add ice cubes and orange slices and serve.

Barbecue Menu

TANDOORI MURGH *Dry Spicy Chicken*	**TABAK MAAS** *Lamb Spare Ribs*	**KAIRI KI CHUTNEY** *Green Mango Chutney*
KALEJI TIKKA *Barbered Liver*	**BHUNA BHUTTA** *Roasted Crown on the Cob*	**SALAAD** *Green Salad*
NIRALE KABABS *Unusual Turkey Kababs*	**BHUNE SAABUT ALOO** *Indian Style Jacket Potatoes*	**MILE JULE TAZE PHAL** *Mixed Fresh Fruit*
SEEKH KABABS *Minced Meat Kababs on Skewers*	**NAAN** *Leavened Bread*	**AAM KI KULFI** *Mango Kulfi*
		VERANDAH PUNCH *A Cool and Refreshing Drink*

Serves ten to twelve people

TANDOORI MURGH
dry spicy chicken

YOU WILL NEED

4 lbs (1kg.800 g) (approximately) spring chicken, skinned; either left whole or in large pieces

FOR RUBBING OVER PRIOR TO MARINADING

2 tbsp lemon juice

1 tsp salt

pinch red food colouring

FOR THE MARINADING MIXTURE (TANDOORI MASALA)

2 tsp coriander seeds

2 tbsp cumin seeds

8 cloves garlic, peeled

2 oz (50 g) fresh root ginger, peeled (fenugreek)

2 tbsp dried methi leaves

2 tbsp fresh mint leaves or 2 tsp dried mint

4 tbsp natural yoghurt

Tandoori chicken is perhaps one of the best loved Indian preparations and ranks high in the world of international cuisine. It is traditionally cooked in a clay oven called a "tandoor"—hence its name tandoori chicken. Here is something that looks great and tastes even better!

Mix lemon juice, salt and colouring and rub this all over the chicken. Keep aside for 15 minutes.

For the marinade mixture (Tandoori masala): Powder the coriander and cumin seeds. Grind the ginger, garlic, mint, coriander and methi leaves.

In a bowl add yoghurt, lemon juice, vinegar and oil. Mix the powdered cumin and coriander seeds and the ginger-garlic mixture and add to the yoghurt. Finally add the salt, chilli powder and colouring and blend thoroughly to form a smooth mixture. It is much easier to prepare this mixture using a food processor. This is your basic "Tandoori masala".

For marinading the chicken: Rub the Tandoori masala thoroughly all over the chicken, not forgetting the cavity, if using full chicken. This is done most effectively by using one's hand rather than a spoon or brush. Leave the chicken to marinate for at least 8 to 12 hrs hours or overnight in the fridge. This helps to tenderize the chicken and allows the spices to penetrate.

Put chicken pieces on grilling racks or on skewers keeping them 8-10 cm away from heat. Barbecue on medium heat basting them with oil a few times until they are cooked through. This can take approximately 10 minutes depending upon the size of the pieces. Take care not to cook too quickly, otherwise the insides will not cook properly.

Contd. ....

4 tbsp fresh green
coriander leaves, chopped

2 tbsp lemon juice

2 tbsp vinegar

2 tbsp mustard oil

2 tsp salt, or to taste

2 tsp chilli powder, or 3
green chillies

1 tsp red food colouring

oil for basting

For best results, bake in a hot oven for 10 minutes or microwave for 3-4 minutes on full power, prior to finishing off on the barbecue.

Handy Hints

1 It not using a barbecue or tandoor this dish can be cooked from start to finish in a medium hot oven (190-200° C/Gas Mark 5-6) for 15-20 minutes, turning the chicken once and baking it uncovered.

2 Tandoori masala can be stored in an air-tight container for 4-5 days in the fridge. It may also be frozen.

3 As the tandoori chicken can be prepared well in advance, it is handy when catering for large numbers.

KALEJI TIKKA
barbecued liver

Liver, with its distinct and unusual flavour, is something of an acquired taste. A good source of iron and a relatively inexpensive cut of meat, we feel it deserves far more prominence. Served as liver shashliks, it is sure to win many a compliment.

YOU WILL NEED

2 lb (900 g) liver, cut into 1 1/2" (4 cm) cubes

2 tsp garlic, minced fine

2 tsp root ginger, minced fine or grated

2 tsp coriander powder

2 tsp salt

1 tsp chilli powder

1 tsp freshly milled black pepper

1 tsp raw dried mango powder (amchur)

2 tbsp vinegar

6 fl oz (150 ml) natural yoghurt

pinch red food colouring (optional)

4 tbsp chopped onions

3 tbsp vegetable oil

Special requirement
Skewers for barbecuing.

Wash and dry the liver pieces.

Liquidize and blend all ingredients from garlic to oil to form a smooth mixture. Apply this to the liver pieces and leave for 1-2 hours.

Thread the liver pieces on to the skewers, leaving a little space between each.

Barbecue, turning and basting the liver pieces with a little of the remaining marinade mixture. Remember liver pieces cook fairly quickly.

Handy Hint
If not barbecuing, heat a little oil in a large frying pan, add the marinaded liver pieces and stir fry for 5-10 minutes, till the mixture is dried and oil begins to separate. This should be done on medium heat.

NIRALE KABAB
unusual turkey kebabs

Although turkey is not frequently consumed in India it is not difficult to find it especially in places where large numbers of Anglo-Indian community reside. These unusual kababs will certainly be that 'extra special' feature on your menu.

You Will Need

2 lb (900 g) turkey breast cut into 1" (2.5 cm) cubes

6 tbsp green coriander leaves

3 tbsp green fenugreek leaves

6 green chillies

2 tbsp garam masala powder

1 tsp dried ginger powder

1 tsp dried garlic powder

2 tsp salt, or to taste

2 tbsp lemon juice

2 tbsp tomato puree

4 tbsp cooking oil

Special requirements
Skewers

Mix all the ingredients from coriander leaves to tomato puree and blend into a smooth mixture. Smear this well over the pork pieces and leave to marinate 6-8 hours or overnight in the fridge.

Thread the pork pieces on the skewers and place them 3-4" (8-10) cms away from the flame, and barbecue till meat is nicely browned. Baste frequently with the leftover marinade. Do not pack the pieces too close together or the adjacent sides will not brown.

Handy Hints
1. Substitute 1 tsp of dry mustard powder for the fresh fenugreek leaves. For a hotter taste, add $^1/_2$ tsp freshly milled black pepper.

2. For those who do not relish turkey, substitute with chicken breast piece. This makes a wonderful change!

3. Do add 1 tbsp of extra cooking oil as the turkey kababs might sometimes appear dry.

SEEKH KABABS
minced meat kababs on skewers

YOU WILL NEED

8 cloves

12 peppercorns

3 tsp coriander seeds

2 tsp cumin seeds

2 tsp poppy seeds (white)

2 oz (70 g) fresh ginger, peeled

2 tsp salt

4 tsp lemon juice

4 tsp vegetable cooking oil or mustard oil

4 tbsp ·natural yoghurt

2 slice of white bread turned into breadcrumbs

2 tbsp dried methi leaves (fenugreek)

4 tbsp fresh coriander leaves, washed and chopped

6 green chillies

Although kababs have their origins in the Middle East, they are very popular in the whole of India, especially in the North.

The word 'seekh' simply means a skewer; and this type of kabab which is grilled on a skewer is called a "seekh kabab .

Kababs may be made either from mince or from small pieces of tender meat, usually lamb. It is quite a common sight in busy marketplaces to see kababs being cooked on open fires, where they permeate the air with their delicious aroma.

Perfect for barbecuing, they may be cooked under a hot grill just as successfully.

Special Requirements
Skewers—approximately 18" (45 cm) long, (pointed at one end only) and about $\frac{1}{2}$" (1 cm) wide in rectangular cross-section.

On a hot griddle, dry roast cloves, peppercorns, coriander, cumin and poppy seeds until they begin to splutter and appear golden in colour. Remove from heat and grind finely.

Liquidize the ginger with salt, lemon juice, cooking oil and natural yoghurt and mix in the breadcrumbs thoroughly.

Mix all the above ingredients into the minced meat and add green coriander leaves and the green chillies. Grind the entire mixture thoroughly. Cover and keep in cool place for at least one hour

Divide mixrture into 20-24 parts Using moistened

164

Contd. ....

2 lb (900 g) minced meat, preferably lamb

palms, wrap each portion of mince around a skewer, by slowly rotating the skewer and pressing down firmly on the meat mixture at the same time; thus encircling the skewer with mince for a length of 6" (15cm) or so. Preheat grill to a high setting and roast the kababs under the grill, turning the skewers around at intervals so that the kababs are browned from all sides. The kababs will come off a skewers very easily once they are cooked.

Serve hot with sirke wale pyaz (onion rings in vinegar) and any chutney.

Handy Hints

1. To save time at the last moment, the mince mixture can be prepared and left overnight in the fridge ready for grilling at the last minute.

2. The seekh kababs may also be cooked ahead and re-heated for a few minutes in a hot oven or in a microwave.

3. These kababs will freeze quite successfully.

4. The kabas can be roasted on a charcoal or electric B.B.Q.

TABAK MAAS
lamb spare ribs

YOU WILL NEED

2 lbs (900 g) spare ribs of lamb

1 tsp turmeric powder

1 tsp chilli powder

2 tsp salt

1 tsp garam masala

16 fl oz (450 ml) water

2 tbsp cooking oil, for basting

These are tender and succulent lamb spare ribs which are a great favourite amongst the people of Kashmir.

In a large pan, place the ribs with all the other ingredients (except oil). Cover and cook on medium heat until the ribs are done. If any water remains, uncover and dry the water off.

Remove ribs from pan, brush with cooking oil and cook over a hot barbecue (or under a hot pre-heated grill) till crisp and browned. Serve hot.

Handy Hint
If a hotter flavour is required, add a teaspoon of freshly milled pepper to the oil, before brushing the chops.

BHUNA BHUTTA
roasted corn on the cob

You Will Need

12 ears of corn

2 lemon, cut into halves

1 tsp salt, or to taste

1 tsp freshly milled black pepper

Corn on the cob being roasted on open charcoal fires by the roadside, especially during the monsoons, is a common sight throughout the whole of India. These are relished by the rich and poor alike and make a convenient snack at any time of the day.

Pull back the green covering leaves and remove the silky strands from the cobs. Place the cobs as near to the heat source (either a barbecue or pre-heated grill) as possible. Keep turning the cobs till a few brown specks appear all over and the corn is cooked.

Remove from heat.

Mix salt and pepper in a small bowl. Dip the lemon halves into the salt and pepper mixture and rub generously all over the corn. Always serve these hot.

Handy Hints

1. When selecting corn on the cobs, choose the youngest, most tender cobs which have a pale colour and are soft when pierced.

2. If desired, rub over the roasted corn with melted butter before serving.

BHUNE SAABUT ALOO
indian style jacket potatoes

YOU WILL NEED

12 medium sized baking potatoes

8 tbsp butter

1 tsp garam masala

1 tsp salt, or to taste

1 tsp chilli powder

1 tsp freshly milled black pepper

$1/2$ tsp rock salt

1 tsp dry roasted cumin seeds, powdered

1 tsp dried mango powder

4 tbsp very fresh coriander leaves, finely chopped

Here is a novel way of barbecuing potatoes.

Special Requirement
Aluminium foil

Wash and scrub potatoes, pierce their skins with a fork, and parboil for 5-10 minutes. Drain and dry them thoroughly and wrap each one loosely in a separate piece of foil. Place in the hot ashes of the barbecue and roast them further until cooked. (Do not use foil if roasting over an electric barbecue.)

Meanwhile, soften butter and mix all the remaining ingredients into it. Remove potatoes from foil. Make a deep slit in each and fill generously with the flavoured butter. Serve hot.

Handy Hint
To vary the flavour fill the potatoes with a mixture of softened butter and green coriander chutney.

NAAN
leavened bread

YOU WILL NEED

2 lb (900 g) plain flour

2 tsp baking powder

$\frac{1}{2}$ oz (15 g) dried yeast
or 1 oz (30 g) fresh yeast

pinch salt

2 tsp sugar

4 fl oz (110 ml) milk

4 fl oz (110 ml) melted ghee

4 eggs, beaten lightly

4 fl oz (110 ml) natural yoghurt

1 tsp nigella seeds

Naans were introduced to the Indian scene centuries ago by the Muslim invaders from the Middle East, but have now become an integral part of Indian cuisine. They are rich, leavened breads, almost always teardrop shaped and traditionally baked in a clay oven. For the sake of convenience, an electric or a gas oven may also be used.

Sift together the flour, baking powder, yeast, salt and sugar in a bowl.

Warm the milk in a saucepan. Remove from heat and add ghee, lightly beaten eggs and yoghurt. Mix thoroughly.

With the help of this mixture (using only as much as is necessary) make a soft, pliable dough. Knead very thoroughly for at least 5 minutes until the dough is smooth and elastic. Form into a ball, brush with a little melted ghee, cover with a damp cloth and leave in a warm place for at least 3 to 4 hours to double in size.

Pre-heat oven to 230°C (Gas mark 8). Knead the dough once again (lightly) and divide it into 16 equal parts. Dust your hands with a little flour and shape each portion into a round.

Take one ball at a time, flatten and roll it into a tear drop shape approximately 9" (23 cm) long and 5" (13 cm) wide. Brush upper surface lightly with water and sprinkle a few nigella seeds over it, pressing them in lightly.

Place 2 (or if space permits, 3) rolled out naans on a baking tray leaving a little space between them. Put them in the pre-heated oven for approximately

169

Contd. ....

5 minutes or until golden spots appear on the surface.

Remove and serve immediately for the best results. However they can also be baked in batches, wrapped in foil and re-heated in a hot oven just before serving.

Handy Hint

Alternatively, the naans may also be cooked under a grill. Pre-heat grill, to its highest setting, and have ready a hot heavy-based griddle, whilst rolling out the naans.

Lightly brush one side of a rolled out naan with water and place the moistened surface on the hot griddle. Brush the top with a little melted ghee and sprinkle some of the nigella seeds over it. When the underside is cooked and golden brown in colour, transfer the naan to the hot grill with the help of a spatula, keeping the nigella side as close as possible to the grill. When the surface acquires brown spots, remove and serve immediately or stack in a clean tea towel to keep warm.

KAIRI KI CHUTNEY
green mango chutney

YOU WILL NEED

4 oz (115 g) raw green mango, peeled and sliced

2 oz (55 g) fresh green coriander leaves

2 green chillies

1 desp sugar

1 tsp salt

1 tbsp onions, peeled and chopped

1-2 tbsp water

Some form of chutney is a necessary accompaniment to every Indian meal. Being piquant in taste, chutneys stimulate the appetite and are believed to promote digestion. Most of them are based on fresh herbs and are uncooked.

Mix all the ingredients together and liquidize. The chutney will keep in the fridge for 3-4 days.

Handy Hint
This chutney freezes well.

MILE JULE TAZE PHAL
mixed fresh fruit

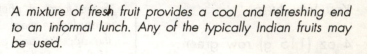

You Will Need

A combination of any of 3 or 4 of the following:

mango skinned, stoned and sliced

papaya skinned, deseeded and sliced or cubed

guava cubed or cut into wedges

lychees peeled and stoned

pineapple sliced or cubed

grapes halved and deseeded

pomegranate outer skin and inner papery membranes removed

apple cored and sliced

peaches stoned and quartered

pears cored and sliced

plums stoned and halved

oranges peeled and cut into segments

A mixture of fresh fruit provides a cool and refreshing end to an informal lunch. Any of the typically Indian fruits may be used.

Prepare fruit. Mix gently, chill and serve.

172

AAM KI KULFI
mango ice-cream

YOU WILL NEED

10 fl oz (280 g) thick double cream

14 oz (410 g) condensed milk

14 oz (390 g) tinned or fresh mango pulp

pinch yellow colouring

FOR GARNISHING

silver leaves

1-2 tbsp pistachios, crushed (optional)

Mango kulfi is not as rich as the ordinary kulfi but has the advantage of having the irresistible flavour of mangoes.

In a large bowl whisk double cream till it is slightly thickened. Add condensed milk and mango pulp and whisk again for 3-4 minutes.

Pour into ice-cream trays, gently cover surface with silver leaves, and sprinkle with crushed pistachios. Freeze for 3-4 hours.

Transfer from freezer compartment into fridge and leave it there for 15-20 minutes before serving. Slice and serve.

Handy Hint
It may also be served with slices of fresh mangoes.

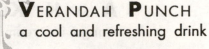

VERANDAH PUNCH
a cool and refreshing drink

YOU WILL NEED

juice of 2 large oranges

juice of 1 thin skinned lemon

200 g sugar

6 fl oz (150 ml) water

10 fl oz (300 ml) freshly made tea, chilled

16 fl oz (450 ml) ginger ale, well chilled

16 fl oz (450 ml) soda water, well chilled

a few ice cubes

thin slices of one large orange for garnishing.

This is a cool and refreshing drink.

Mix together the fruit juices, sugar, water, and tea. Cool and strain into a bowl and chill. Just before serving mix in the ginger ale and soda water. Add ice cubes and orange slices and serve.

Cocktail Menu

BHAJIAS *Savoury Vegetable Fritters*	**TALE PAAPAD** *Fried Poppadums*	**SUGGESTED DRINKS**
SAMOSAS *Pastry Filled with Peas and Potatoes*	**BHARE KHAJOOR** *Stuffed Cocktail Dates*	**TAMATAR KA RAS** *Tomato Juice Indian Style*
MACHLI KABABS *Fish Kababs*	**PHALON KI CHAAT** *Indian Style Fresh Fruit Salad*	**TARBOOZ KI SHARBAT** *Watermelon Sherbet*
RESHMI KABABS *Grilled Chicken Kababs*	**ANOKHI CHUTNEY** *Sweet and Sour Chutney*	**NIMBU PAANI** *Sweet/Savoury Fresh Lime Drink*
MASALEDAR KAJU *Devilled Cashewnuts*	**DAHI PUDINA** *Yoghurt and Mint Dip*	

Serves four to six people

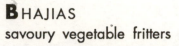

BHAJIAS
savoury vegetable fritters

On many a footpath in India one comes across vendors selling sizzling hot bhajias—an ever popular snack. Bhajias are vegetable fritters coated in gram flour batter which gives them their characteristic colour and taste.

YOU WILL NEED

FOR THE BATTER

6 oz (170 g) gram flour

$^1/_2$ tsp chilli powder

1 tsp salt, or to taste

$^1/_2$ tsp garam masala powder

$^1/_2$ tsp dried mango powder or 1 tsp lemon juice

1 tbsp fresh green coriander

leaves, finely chopped

$^1/_2$ tsp thymol seeds (optional)

5 fl oz (150 ml) warm water (approximately)

1 tbsp warmed oil

VEGETABLES

2 medium sized potatoes, peeled and thinly sliced into rounds (about 1.5 cm thick)

To make the batter
Sieve the gram flour into a bowl and add salt, chilli powder, garam masala powder, dried mango powder or lemon juice, thymol seeds (if using) and chopped coriander leaves. Mix and pour in the warm water slowly, beating the mixture thoroughly until a dropping consistency is reached. Add the hot oil and beat further. Cover and leave aside for 10 - 15 minutes.

Meanwhile prepare the vegetables and set the oil to heat in a kadhai/wok/deep frying pan and bring it to near smoking point. Drop the vegetable pieces into the batter a few at a time, and coat them well. Then shake off any excess batter and carefully drop them into the hot oil. Fry small batchfuls over medium heat, until golden brown in colour, turning them over once. Do not brown them too quickly or else the vegetables might not get fully cooked.

Remove and drain on kitchen paper. Serve hot with tomato ketchup, or green coriander chutney.

Alternate method
Instead of slicing the potatoes and onions into rounds, cut them into dice (no bigger than 1 cm cube).

Make a stiff batter using less warm water and add $^1/_4$ tsp baking powder. Add the diced vegetables and mix thoroughly (consistency resembling that of a rich fruit cake batter).

Contd. ....

2 medium sized onions, peeled and sliced into rounds (about 1 cm thick)

vegetable oil for deep frying

Deep fry spoonfuls (desp) of the batter on medium heat in small batches until cooked through and golden brown.

Handy Hint

A variety of vegetables may be used for making the bhajias, e.g., small pieces of cauliflower, aubergines, chopped spinach etc.

SAMOSAS
potatoes and peas pastry parcels

Samosas are deep fried pastry parcels with various fillings. They are great as snacks or even as part of a main meal. Although they take a little time to prepare, the end result is always rewarding.

You Will Need

For The Filling

6 oz (170 g) peeled and cooked potatoes

2 oz (55 g) cooked peas

1 oz (30 g) finely chopped onions

2 finely chopped green chillies

1 tbsp chopped coriander leaves

1 tsp garam masala

1 tsp mango powder or lemon juice

1 tsp salt, or to taste

$^{1}/_{2}$ tsp roasted cumin seed powder

For The Pastry

5 oz (150 g) plain flour

1 fl oz (30 ml) cooking oil for rubbing into the flour

To make the filling
Roughly mash the potatoes and add all the ingredients from the peas to the cumin seeds. Mix well and keep aside.

To make the pastry
Sieve together the flour and salt, rub in the cooking oil and add just enough water to knead into a stiff but smooth dough. Divide the dough into approximately 10 pieces. Knead thoroughly, cover with a damp cloth and leave to rest for 10-15 minutes.

Divide the dough into 5 pieces and shape them into balls. With the help of a little dry flour roll out each ball into a circle about 5-6" (10-12 cm) in diameter and 2 mm thick.

Cut each circle into half, moisten the edges of each semi-circle and press the straight edges together to form a cone. Fill the cone with the prepared stuffing and seal the remaining edges by pressing them together. Finish filling all the samosas in this way, cover with a tea towel and keep aside.

To fry the samosas
Heat the cooking oil in a kadhai/deep frying pan. Reduce to medium heat and fry 3 to 4 samosas at a time until pale golden brown on all sides. Remove and drain them on a kitchen towel. Serve immediately with a green coriander chutney or any other chutney of your choice.

pinch salt

a little water to make a stiff dough

vegetable oil for deep frying

Handy Hint

1 To re-heat, place uncovered in a hot oven for 4-5 minutes, or re-fry quickly in hot oil. Avoid microwaving as this makes the pastry soggy.

2. Readymade filo pastry can be substituted for the home-made pastry.

MACHLI KABAB
fish kabab

These fish kababs will no doubt be a hit at your next cocktail party!

YOU WILL NEED

1 lb (450 g) cod fillets or any firm fleshed white fish

1 tsp lemon juice

1 tsp salt, or to taste

1 tbsp finely chopped coriander leaves

2 finely chopped and deseeded green chillies

$1/4$" (0.5 cm) peeled and grated ginger

pinch freshly ground black pepper

2 tbsp breadcrumbs

1 egg, lightly beaten

oil for deep frying

Steam the fish lightly, remove skin and all bones. Fork the flesh gently and mix in the rest of the ingredients except the oil. Divide the mixture into walnut-sized balls and deep fry in batches on medium heat until golden in colour. Drain and serve hot with any sauce or chutney of your choice.

Handy Hints

1. The fish mixture can be prepared in advance and left in the fridge ready for frying.

2. To re-heat the fried fish kababs, either place uncovered in a hot oven for a few minutes or re-fry in hot oil very briefly.

RESHMI KABAB
grilled chicken kebabs

YOU WILL NEED

1 lb (450 g) chicken breast, boned, skinned and cut into 2" (5 cm) pieces

1 tsp minced ginger

1 tsp minced garlic

1 tbsp chopped coriander leaves

2 tsp chopped green chillies

1 tsp salt or to taste

1 egg

large pinch saffron or yellow food colouring

1 tbsp extra-thick cream

Reshmi kababs are succulent, tender pieces of marinated chicken that simply melt in the mouth. A must for any cocktail party.

Special Requirements
Thick skewers

Grind together the ginger, garlic, coriander leaves, green chillies and salt with the help of very little water to form a smooth mixture. Marinate the chicken pieces in this mixture and leave to refrigerate for a few hours or better still, overnight.

When ready to grill, add the lightly beaten egg, saffron (dissolved in a tsp of water) and the cream. Mix into the chicken thoroughly. Thread the chicken pieces onto the skewers leaving a little gap between each piece. Place under a hot grill and keep turning them in order to cook and brown evenly. Serve immediately while they are sizzling hot.

Handy Hint
Reshmi kababs can be frozen successfully. To reheat either microwave or defrost at room temperature and place in a hot oven for 2-3 minutes.

MASALEDAR KAJU
devilled cashewnuts

YOU WILL NEED

1 tsp cooking oil

8 oz (225 g) whole cashewnuts (unsalted)

1/4 tsp sea salt/rock salt preferably, or table salt

1/4 tsp freshly ground black pepper

1/4 tsp dried mango powder

1/4 tsp chilli powder, optional

A variety of nuts lightly spiced and fried are commonly served in Indian homes as snacks. Cashewnuts, being expensive, are really a luxury. And, be warned, these are so tasty that one can't stop eating them.

Heat the oil in a heavy-based pan, reduce heat and fry cashewnuts to a very pale golden colour. Stir them continuously while frying in order to get an even colour. Remove from heat, add the rest of the ingredients and mix well. Cool and store in an airtight container.

Handy Hints

1. Use almonds with skins instead of cashewnuts.

2. Shelled peanuts can be an economical alternative.

3. Another way to spice the nuts is to mix all the ingredients together, spread out evenly on a plate and microwave on full power for 2 minutes. Cool and store.

TALE PAAPAD
fried poppadums

YOU WILL NEED

4-6 paapads

vegetable cooking oil for deep frying

a pair of tongs

Most people buy their paapads readymade. Both plain and variously spiced kinds are readily available. All that is needed then is to cook them, just before eating. Paapads should be crisp when served.

Set a kadhai or deep frying pan over medium heat with the cooking oil. When hot, immerse a paapad completely in the hot oil. Within seconds it will swell and rise to the surface. Its cooking is complete. It should be removed immediately (as it will otherwise burn very quickly) using the tongs, and left to drain on kitchen paper.

Repeat until all the paapads are done.

There should be enough room in the pan for the paapads to swell. Some almost double in size, so if necessary, cut them into halves or quarters before frying.

BHARE HUE KHAJOOR
cocktail dates

Plenty of dates grow in India although few people there appreciate them fully. Dried dates stuffed with cashewnuts are an interesting and unusual item to serve.

YOU WILL NEED

12-16 dried dates

12-16 whole cashewnuts

2 tbsp unsweetened desiccated coconut

2 tps finely chopped walnuts and pistachio

12-16 cocktail sticks

Slit the dates and carefully remove the stones. Replace these with whole cashewnuts, press firmly and re-shape the dates. In a polythene bag place the coconut, walnuts and pistachios and drop the stuffed whole dates into the bag. Gently shake the dates so that they are thoroughly coated with the mixture. Remove the dates from the bag and serve on a plate with cocktail sticks.

Handy Hint
Sometimes the dates do not have a sticky surface and it is easier to coat them by putting the nut mixture in a small bowl and one by one dipping each date and pressing the mixture lightly on to them.

PHALON KI CHAAT
indian style fresh fruit salad

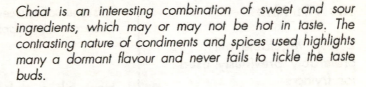

Chaat is an interesting combination of sweet and sour ingredients, which may or may not be hot in taste. The contrasting nature of condiments and spices used highlights many a dormant flavour and never fails to tickle the taste buds.

YOU WILL NEED

1 lb 450 g mixed fresh fruit—e.g., a combination of 4 or 5 fruits chosen from the following: guava, banana, orange, papaya, apple, grapes, pineapple, watermelon or pomegranate

1 tbsp lemon juice

pinch red chilli powder

pinch freshly milled black pepper

$1/4$ tsp salt

$1/4$ tsp (black) rock salt

$1/2$ tsp roasted, and powdered cumin seeds

Prepare fruit into bite-sized pieces. Mix the rest of the ingredients together and pour over prepared fruit. Mix gently: cover and chill for half an hour before serving. Do not leave for much longer as the fruit juices might begin to run.

ANOKHI CHUTNEY
an unusual chutney

YOU WILL NEED

2 tbsp vegetable oil, preferably previously used for frying

6 oz (170 g) spring onions, finely minced

4 oz (115 g) fresh green coriander leaves, finely chopped

2 oz (55 g) ginger, scraped and finely minced

1 oz (30 g) garlic, skinned and finely minced

4-6 green chillies

2 tbsp soya sauce

$\frac{1}{2}$ tsp freshly ground black pepper

1 tsp salt

4 tbsp chilli sauce, or to taste

This unusual chutney with its origins in the Far East, has been cleverly adapted to suit the Indian palate.

Heat oil in a frying pan and add spring onions, ginger, garlic, green coriander, and green chillies. Fry for a minute or so but be careful not to let them brown. Add soya sauce, black pepper, salt and chilli sauce. Remove from heat, mix well, cool and serve.

Handy Hints
1. If kept in an air-tight jar, it will keep three to four days or more in the fridge.

2. If a less pungent taste is required substitute tomato ketchup for chilli sauce.

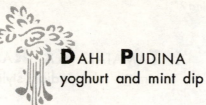

DAHI PUDINA
yoghurt and mint dip

You Will Need

5 fl oz (150 ml) thick set natural yoghurt

1 tbsp bottled mint or a handful of freshly ground mint leaves

$\frac{1}{2}$ tsp salt

Nothing can be simpler than this instant dip.

Blend all the ingredients together in a bowl. Chill, and serve garnished with a couple of fresh mint leaves.

Serve as a dip/chutney/accompaniment to the savoury items within the menu.

TAMATAR KA RAS
tomato juice indian style

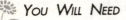

YOU WILL NEED

2 large ripe tomatoes, chopped roughly

25 fl oz (750 ml) water

1/4 tsp freshly milled pepper

4 tsp sugar

1/2 tsp black rock salt or sea salt

4-6 mint leaves

a few ice cubes

Fresh tomato juice is a marvellous drink and is a favourite especially with ladies and teetotallers.

Liquidize the tomatoes with water and rub through a sieve. Add sugar and salt and mix thoroughly. Leave to chill for an hour or two.

To serve—place a few ice cubes in a glass, top up with the prepared tomato juice, sprinkle freshly milled pepper and garnish with a couple of mint leaves.

Handy Hint
If a thicker consistency is required, then use only half the amount of water.

TARBOOZ KI SHARBAT
watermelon sherbet

YOU WILL NEED

2 ¹/₂ lbs (675 g) watermelon

4 fl oz (150 ml) water

1 tbsp castor sugar

pinch salt

4 oz (100 g) crushed ice cubes

large pinch dried ginger powder

Tarbooz ki sharbat is a cool, light and refreshing drink which looks as good as it tastes.

Remove the tough outer skin and deseed the watermelon. Scoop out 10-12 balls and save them for the garnish.

Place all the ingredients (except ginger powder and scooped out watermelon balls) in a liquidizer and liquidize for 2 minutes. Check seasoning and add more sugar if required.

Chill and serve in tall glasses topped with watermelon balls and sprinkle lightly with dry ginger powder.

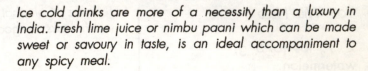

NIMBU PAANI
fresh lime drink

YOU WILL NEED

2 ¹/₂ fl oz (75 ml) juice of
freshly squeezed lime or
lemon

30 fl oz (900 ml) water

1 oz (30 g) castor sugar
or 1 tsp salt, according to
taste

rock salt

ice cubes

TO GARNISH:

lime or lemon slices

Ice cold drinks are more of a necessity than a luxury in India. Fresh lime juice or nimbu paani which can be made sweet or savoury in taste, is an ideal accompaniment to any spicy meal.

Mix lime or lemon juice, water, sugar/salt and rock salt thoroughly. Serve with ice cubes and a twist of lime or lemon slices.

Handy Hints

1. For that little extra touch, add a few mint leaves as garnish.

2. A sprinkling of freshly ground black pepper can further add to the flavour.

Informal Tea Menu

KHEEME KA SAMOSA
Deep Fried Pastry Parcels
Filled with Mince

POHE
Savoury Flaked Rice Snack

SOOJI KA HALWA
Rich Semolina Dessert

PISTA NAAN KHATAI
Indian Pistachio Cookies

NARIYAL KI CHUTNEY
Coconut Chutney

KADHI HUI CHAI
Strong, Brewed Tea

Serves four to six people

KHEEME KA SAMOSA
deep fried pastry parcels filled with mince

Kheeme ka samosa is a deep fried pastry envelope filled with minced lamb and is quite delicious with a wonderfully meaty taste.

YOU WILL NEED

FOR THE PASTRY

5 oz (150 g) plain flour

pinch salt

1 fl oz (30 ml) cooking oil for rubbing into the flour

sufficient water to make a stiff dough

FOR THE FILLING

1 tbsp cooking oil

1-2 cloves

1-2 green cardamoms

1 oz (30 g) onions, skinned and finely chopped

8 oz (225 g) lean lamb, minced

2 oz (55 g) shelled peas

¹/₂ (1.25")fresh ginger, peeled and grated

1 clove garlic

For the pastry
Sieve together the flour and salt in a bowl, rub in the cooking oil and add just sufficient water to form a stiff dough. Knead thoroughly until smooth, then cover and allow it to rest for about 10 minutes.

To prepare the filling
Heat the oil in a saucepan and when hot add the cloves and cardamoms. Stir for a few seconds, then add the onions and fry them until golden brown. Next add all the remaining ingredients except the lemon juice and green coriander leaves to the pan, and fry gently for a few minutes until the mince is browned. Cover and cook on medium heat until the mince is cooked and all the liquid released from it has dried off. (Add a little water if necessary for the mince to cook.)

Remove from heat, add the coriander leaves and lemon juice and mix well. Check and adjust seasoning if necessary. Allow the mince to cool before filling samosas i.e., the pastry envelopes.

Filling and frying the samosas
Divide the dough into approximately 5 portions and shape each one into a ball. Flatten and roll each one out (with the help of a little dry flour) into a circle of about 4" (10 cm) in diameter, then cut it into half. Take each semi-circle, moisten the straight edge with a little water and make it into a cone by folding and

192

Contd. ....

1-2 green chillies, finely chopped

$\frac{1}{2}$ tsp garam masala powder

$\frac{1}{2}$ tsp salt, or to taste

1 tbsp chopped fresh coriander leaves

1 tsp lemon or lime juice

pressing the moistened edge together. Fill with the cooked mince, moisten the inside of the cone rim with a little water and press opposite sides together to seal, forming a triangular parcel. Fill all the samosas in this way and keep covered to prevent the pastry from drying.

Heat the cooking oil in a kadhai or deep frying pan and when hot, slide in 3-4 samosas (so as not to overcrowd the frying pan) at a time and deep fry for about 5 minutes until pale golden brown, turning them once. Remove with a slotted spoon and drain on kitchen paper. Serve hot with any green chutney.

Handy Hint

Generally the size of kheeme ke samose, especially if they are meant to be served with drinks is quite small (about half the size of aloo ka samosa). In any case, this is a matter of individual choice, and for the sake of expediency, their size, as described in the procedure above, has not been reduced.

POHE
savoury flaked rice snack

You Will Need

80 oz (225 g) flaked rice

1 tsp salt, or to taste

1/2 tsp sugar

1-2 tbsp water

4 tbsp vegetable cooking oil

1 tsp small black mustard seeds

few curry leaves

3 oz (85 g) onions, peeled and finely minced

3 oz (85 g) potatoes, peeled and diced into 1/2" (1 cm) cubes

3 oz (85 g) cooked peas

4 green chillies, deseeded and sliced fine

2/3 tsp turmeric powder

1 tbsp fresh green coriander leaves, finely chopped

1 tbsp lemon juice

1 tbsp desiccated coconut

It is interesting to note that rice can also be turned into delicious snacks or sweetmeats. This appetizing savoury flaked rice dish makes a light yet filling tea time snack.

Place the flaked rice in a bowl and mix in salt and sugar. Sprinkle water and toss the rice so that the grains are evenly moistened. (Use a little more water if necessary.)

In a deep, heavy pan or kadhai heat oil. Add mustard seeds and curry leaves. When seeds begin to splutter, add onions and potatoes. Fry for a few minutes till potatoes are barely tender. Add peas and green chillies, and reduce heat. Keep stirring gently till vegetables are cooked. Add turmeric powder and fry further for a few seconds.

Now add the moistened flaked rice and gently but thoroughly mix all the ingredients together. Add coriander leaves, mix again and cover immediately. Cook on very low heat for 2-3 minutes. Remove from heat and leave covered for a further 2-3 minutes.

Just before serving, sprinkle lemon juice. Turn out pohe into a serving dish and garnish with desiccated coconut.

Handy Hints
1. If desired, you could add tiny cauliflower florets, finely sliced french beans and carrots.

2. A nutty version of pohe can be served by omitting all vegetables and substituting a variety of nuts instead.

SOOJI KA HALWA
rich semolina dessert

YOU WILL NEED

large pinch saffron

5 oz (150 g) sugar

10 fl oz (300 ml) water

6 green cardamoms, crushed

5 oz (150 g) ghee

5 oz (150 g) coarse semolina

a few drops yellow food colouring

2 tbsp slivered almonds, or a mixture of chopped nuts (e.g., almonds, cashewnuts) and raisins

Sooji ka halwa is amongst the few Indian sweets which does not use milk in its preparation. It is, however, a rather sweet, and rich dish due to the generous amount of ghee which goes into its making.

Soak the saffron in 1 tsp of water. Boil the sugar and water along with the cardamoms for 2-3 minutes in order to make the syrup.

Set the kadhai or wok on medium heat and heat a quarter of the ghee in it. Stir in the semolina and very gradually and with constant stirring, let it turn a pale golden brown. This requires a little patience to get good results as the semolina needs to be browned evenly and slowly.

When the semolina is golden in colour, gently add the syrup, saffron, food colouring and the slivered almonds (or the nuts and raisins), taking care to keep stirring vigorously all the time. This constant stirring is important in order to avoid the formation of lumps. When the mixture starts to leave the sides of the kadhai, add the rest of the ghee and stir well.

Remove the halwa from the heat and transfer to a serving bowl. Always serve the halwa warm as it then tastes far nicer.

Handy Hints

1. If a less rich halwa is desired, the amount of ghee used may be reduced by as much as half.

2. The food colouring only serves to enhance the appearance of the halwa and can be omitted without affecting the taste.

PISTA NAAN KHATAI
indian pistachio cookies

YOU WILL NEED

7 oz (200 g) castor sugar

7 oz (200 g) fine semolina

7 oz (200 g) plain flour

7 fl oz (210 g) warmed and liquified ghee (preferably) or vegetable cooking oil

3 ½ oz (100 g) gram flour

½ tsp baking powder

½ tsp soda bicarbonate

10 green cardamoms, shelled and seeds powdered

1 oz (30 g) almonds, ground

2 oz (60 g) unsalted pistachios, ground or roughly chopped

21 tbsp finely chopped pistachios for garnishing (optional)

There is no great tradition of home baking in Indian households and relatively few homes have electric ovens. Many a housewife gets her odd baking done at the corner bake-shop which is quite happy to do so for a small charge. Thus occasionally one sees people carrying all the raw, weighed up ingredients to the baker's and returning with the finished products. Naan khatais are a popular tea time snack and are the equivalent of Western cookies.

Pre-heat the oven to 100ºC (Gas Mark 5).

In a large bowl, place all the ingredients (except the pistachios for garnishing) and mix to form a dough-like consistency. There is no need to add water or milk.

Make walnut-sized balls, but do not flatten them. Space these out on a greased baking tray and place a large pinch of chopped pistachios on each ball as a garnish. Bake until golden brown for approximately 10-15 minutes. Cool and store in an air-tight jar.

Handy Hint
To make plain naan khatais, substitute an equal weight of plain flour for the almonds and pistachios.

NARIYAL KI CHUTNEY
coconut chutney

YOU WILL NEED

¹/₂ fresh coconut, coarsely grated (preferably) or 4 oz (115 g) coarsely desiccated coconut

4 fl oz (120 ml) natural yoghurt

1 level tsp salt, or to taste

1 tsp vegetable cooking oil

¹/₂ tsp split black gram (urad dal)

2-3 small red chillies

¹/₂ tsp small black mustard seeds

5-6 curry leaves

Nariyal ki chutney goes well with almost any snack. The taste of fresh coconut is unbeatable and it is certainly worth the effort finding one.

Thoroughly mix the grated coconut, yoghurt and salt and keep aside in a serving bowl.

Heat oil in a small saucepan and add the black gram, red chillies, mustard seeds and curry leaves. As soon as the seeds splutter, remove from heat and pour the entire contents over the coconut yoghurt mixture.

Mix gently and serve. Remember to remove the chillies before eating.

Handy Hint
To enhance the flavour, run the prepared chutney for a few seconds in a liquidizer.

KADHI HUI CHAI
strong, well brewed tea

YOU WILL NEED

2 pints (1.2 litres) water

3-4 tea bags or 3-4 tsp tea-dust tied loosely in a muslin bag

3 tbsp sugar, or to taste

5 fl oz (150 ml) boiled milk

2 tbsp extra thick cream

This is the kind of tea that can be bought off the many small tea-stalls found in every corner of India. A combination of tea-dust, sugar and water is gently brewed for hours on end and served with boiled milk or a dollop of fresh cream at extra cost! Such tea is commonly served in unglazed earthen cups which impart their unique earthy fragrance— altogether an unforgettable experience.

Bring the water to boil in a saucepan. Reduce heat to low and add sugar and tea. Simmer the tea very gently until almost $1/4$ of the water evaporates.

Boil the milk separately. To serve, pour the brewed tea into cups, top with the required amount of boiling milk and thick cream (optional).

Handy Hint
To vary: add 1 tsp aniseed along with the sugar when brewing the tea.

Formal Tea Menu

TANGRI KABAB
Chicken Drumsticks

PANEER PAKORA
Cheese Fritters

PUFF PASTRY

**GARMA-GARAM
CHEESE KE SANDWICH**
*Toasted Cheese
Sandwiches*

NIMKI
Savoury niblets

SOOKHI SEVIYAAN
Sweet Vermicelli

CAKE
Eggless Cake

**TAMATAR AUR
LAHSUN KI CHUTNEY**
Tomato And Garlic Chutney

DARJEELING CHAI
Darjeeling Tea

Serves six to eight people

TANGRI KABAB
chicken drumsticks

Tangri kabab is an uncomplicated preparation of marinated chicken drumsticks which are grilled. It is a versatile dish which can be served either as part of a main meal or with afternoon tea.

YOU WILL NEED

8 medium chicken drumsticks

2 tbsp yoghurt

1" (2.5 cm) fresh ginger, scraped

2 cloves garlic, peeled

2 green chillies, or to taste

1 tsp salt

1 tsp cumin seeds

1 tbsp gram flour

1 tbsp lemon juice

1 tsp garam masala powder

a few drops red or yellow colouring

FOR GARNISH

onion rings and lemon wedges

Skin, wash and dry the drumsticks. Make deep lengthwise cuts.

Grind all the remaining ingredients into a smooth mixture and marinate the drumsticks in it for 5-6 hours or overnight in the fridge.

Pre-heat the oven to a high setting: 230ºC (Gas mark 8) and bake the drumsticks for about 10 minutes. Finish off under a hot pre-heated grill for 2-3 minutes, turning them once.

Serve hot, garnished with onion rings and lemon wedges.

Handy Hint
Tangri kababs are ideally suited for barbecues too.

PANEER PAKORA
cheese fritters

These much sought after tasty morsels have a more subtle flavour than ordinary pakoras and are indeed a real treat.

YOU WILL NEED

FOR THE BATTER

6 oz (150 g) gram flour

1 tsp salt, or to taste

$^1/_2$ tsp red chilli powder

$^1/_2$ tsp thymol (ajwain) seeds

1 tbsp warmed vegetable cooking oil

5 fl oz (150 ml) warm water or as required

6 oz (170 g) paneer/ tofu pieces cut into $^3/_4$" x 1 $^1/_2$" pieces (2 cm x 5 cm)

To make the batter
Sieve the gram flour along with the salt and red chilli powder into a bowl.

Add thymol seeds and warmed oil and mix well. Gradually add enough warm water to make a smooth batter of dropping consistency. Cover and leave aside for 10-15 minutes.

To make the pakoras
If using tofu, wash it well under running water. Drain and dry thoroughly with kitchen paper.

Heat oil in a deep frying pan. Dip the paneer/tofu pieces in the prepared batter, ensure that they are thoroughly coated and fry them in batches until crisp and golden brown, turning them once to ensure even cooking. Remove with a slotted spoon, drain on absorbent paper and serve hot.

These pakoras go very well with tomato-garlic chutney.

Handy Hint
To vary the flavour, omit the thymol seeds and add 1 heaped tablespoon of fresh chopped green coriander and 2-3 finely cut green chillies to the batter.

PUFF PASTRY

YOU WILL NEED

8 oz (225 g) plain flour

8 oz (225 g) unsalted butter

5 fl oz (150 ml) chilled water—just $\frac{1}{2}$ tbsp less (approximately)

$\frac{1}{2}$ tbsp lemon juice

Puff pastry: Puff pastry is fiddly and time-consuming to prepare, and that's the main reason why people prefer to use readymade puff pastry. However, if it is not available here is a quick recipe for it.

Cut the butter into $\frac{1}{2}$ oz (10 g) pieces.

Sift the flour and salt into a bowl, and add the pieces of butter. Very gently, just toss them about to coat them with flour, but do not 'mix' or 'work' the pastry in yet.

Make a well in the centre and pour in the iced water mixed with the lemon juice. Using a palette knife make numerous cuts across the flour mixture, turning the bowl around as you do so, in order to gently bring all the ingredients together. Work quickly, and as soon as you have a reasonable lump of the mixture, turn it out onto floured board—along with all the loose flour that might be left.

Lightly shape the mixture into a rectangular block, using your hands. Now take a large rolling pin, and holding it right at the ends, make three quick depressions widthwise to trap the air. Now roll out the pastry into an oblong approximately 7"x 4", again holding the rolling pin at the ends—to avoid pressure directly over the pastry.

Fold one third of the rolled pastry over the centre and do the same with the other end. Press down the edges firmly with the rolling pin and rest the pastry for 5 minutes.

Lift the pastry, and flour the board. Then give the

Contd. ....

pastry a quick quarter turn, and make three brisk depressions as before with the rolling pin. Repeat the whole process three more times, remembering to keep the rolling pin and board well floured throughout.

Cover the pastry well with polythene or aluminium foil and chill thoroughly in the fridge for several hours, preferably overnight.

Allow pastry to come back to room temperature before rolling it out for filling.

Handy Hints

1. The mince filling can be made well in advance and frozen—ready for use after thawing whenever required.

2. Curry puffs freeze quite well and are a useful standby for picnics etc.

3. To re-heat, it is best to place them in a hot oven for a few minutes. (Microwaving is not recommended as it makes the pastry soft rather than crisp.)

GARMA-GARAM CHEESE KE SANDWICHES
toasted cheese sandwiches

YOU WILL NEED

12 medium slices of white bread

1 oz (25 g) butter

3 oz (75 g) grated cheese

2 ripe tomatoes

2 oz (50 g) finely sliced onions or chopped spring onions

2 green chillies, finely chopped

pinch salt and freshly milled black pepper

sandwich toaster (lightly greased on the inside)

Nothing like a toasted sandwich when one is feeling hungry! This is a versatile item which can serve the purpose of either a quick snack on its own or be part of a whole menu.

Butter all slices of bread. Keep six slices, buttered side down, and sprinkle cheese generously. Top with slices of tomato, onions and green chillies. Sprinkle a little freshly milled pepper and a little salt. Cover with the remaining slices (buttered side face up).

Place in sandwich toaster, and allow to cook for 2-3 minutes. Remove and serve hot with a little green salad.

Handy Hint

Any filling of your choice, cooked vegetarian or non-vegetarian, can be used e.g., bhuna kheema.

Nimki Or Namak Pare
savoury niblets

You Will Need

8 oz (225 g) plain flour

$^3/_4$ tsp salt

2 tbsp vegetable cooking oil

$^3/_4$ tsp thymol seeds

$^1/_4$ tsp freshly milled black pepper

2 fl oz (50 ml) (approximately) water

1 oz (30 g) extra dry flour for rolling out

vegetable cooking oil for deep frying

These are simple yet appetizing savouries with a mild flavour. They are usually diamond shaped and keep well for several weeks in an air-tight container.

Sieve the flour with salt in a large bowl. Rub in the cooking oil and add thymol seeds and pepper. Mix well. Add sufficient water gradually and knead thoroughly to form a stiff dough. Let it rest for 10-15 minutes. Divide the dough into 2 portions.

Take each portion in turn and roll it out into a thick circle about $^1/_8$" (0.25 cm) in thickness. Use the extra dry flour, if needed. Prick the surface with a fork and using a sharp knife make parallel cuts about $^1/_2$" (0.5 cm) wide. Now make similar parallel cuts again but this time at a slight angle (45°) from the original so as to finish with a diamond cut.

Heat vegetable cooking oil in a kadhai/wok or deep frying pan. Put in 1 or 2 handfuls of the rolled and cut out dough (do not overcrowd the frying pan) and fry the nimkis to a pale golden colour on gentle heat. The slower the frying, the crisper will be the end result. Remove the nimkis with a slotted spoon, and drain on kitchen paper. Repeat the above process until all the nimkis have been fried.

When cool, store in an air-tight container.

Handy Hints

1. If you do not like the flavour of thymol seeds, simply omit them altogether, or, if desired, substitute with nigella seeds.

2. Substitute red chilli powder for black pepper, or omit them both if you wish.

SOOKHI SEVIYAAN
sweet vermicelli

Sookhi seviyaan are perhaps the simplest of sweet preparations, yet are a suitable choice for serving with afternoon tea.

YOU WILL NEED

3 oz (85 g) ghee

2 green cardamoms

6 oz (170 g) vermicelli, fine quality

1 tbsp chopped cashewnuts

1 tbsp chopped almonds

1 tbsp small green sultanas

3 oz (85 g) sugar

6 fl oz (180 ml) warm water

large pinch saffron (optional)

Heat ghee in a wide pan. Add the crushed cardamoms and after a few seconds, stir in the vermicelli and fry it on low heat until rich brown in colour. (Take care as it tends to brown rather quickly.) Add the chopped nuts, sultanas and sugar and stir for a further minute or so.

Next add the warm water and saffron (if using it) and mix gently so as not to break up the vermicelli too much. Cover and cook for 3-5 minutes. The vermicelli strands should absorb all the liquid. If some liquid remains, uncover, increase the heat and dry off the remaining liquid (thus preventing it from becoming mushy).

Serve immediately, piled in a deep bowl. To re-heat, either place it in a microwave or re-heat in a pan with a few tablespoons of boiling water.

Handy Hint

Soft brown sugar may be used for a slightly different flavour, in which case use 2 oz (60 g) soft brown sugar during the cooking and sprinkle 1 oz (30 g) of it over the cooked seviyaan just before serving.

Eggless Cake

You Will Need

1 lb (450 g) self raising flour

8 oz (225 g) margarine

8 oz (225 g) sugar

2 tbsp custard powder

2 tbsp vinegar

1 tsp baking powder

1 tsp bicarbonate of soda

½ pint (300 ml) milk

2 tbsp mixed and chopped dried fruit

This cake recipe is somewhat different in that it does not use eggs, but vinegar.

Pre-heat oven to 160°C (Gas Mark 3)

Sieve the flour into a large bowl and rub in the margarine. Add sugar, custard powder and fruit (optional) and mix well.

Pour the vinegar into a jug and add the baking powder and soda bicarbonate (this is the raising agent). Add the milk gradually and mix into the flour. Place mixture into a pre-greased, lined tin.

Bake in the centre of the oven for 1 hour. Remove cake from oven, cover with foil then put back in the oven for 1 more hour.

Cool slightly before removing from the tin.

TAMATAR AUR LAHSUN KI CHUTNEY
tomato and garlic chutney

This tomato and garlic chutney has a sweet and sour taste and will easily keep for a week or so in the fridge.

YOU WILL NEED

¹/₂ lb (225 g) tomatoes

1-2 green chillies or to taste, chopped fine

1 tsp garlic paste

1 level tsp salt, or to taste

1 tbsp sugar

8-10 tbsp water

4 tbsp vinegar

Scald the tomatoes, remove skin, and chop into small pieces.

Set a heavy-based saucepan over medium heat and place the chopped tomatoes, green chillies and garlic paste along with the water and cook until soft and pulpy.

Add salt and sugar and cook for a few minutes until the mixture thickens and acquires a glazed appearance.

Remove from heat, add vinegar, mix thoroughly and store in an air-tight jar in the fridge.

DARJEELING CHAI
darjeeling tea

YOU WILL NEED

2 pints (1.25 litres) boiling water

5 tsp Darjeeling tea leaves or 3 tea bags

Darjeeling tea is amongst the finest grown in the world.

Whilst nothing could be simpler than making tea, it is worth following a few basic rules.

Always boil the water freshly and preferably in a non-aluminium pan.

Always use fresh tap water and boil it in a stainless steel pan or kettle (not aluminium).

Remember to warm up the tea pot first before putting in the tea leaves/bags and pouring boiling water over it. Stir, and immediately replace the lid and cover the tea pot with a tea cosy. Leave it for 3-4 minutes for the tea to brew. Stir it once again before straining it out into the tea-cups. Serve with or without sugar according to taste.

WELL LOVED TWO DISH COMBINATIONS

Certain items of food such as 'fish and chips', 'bangers and mash' etc., when served together always seems to go hand in hand and complement each other perfectly. The inclusion of any further dishes along with these, although welcome, is really not required. The appeal of such combinations lies in their very simplicity and uncomplicated nature.

Almost every cuisine from the four corners of the earth has its own such favourite combinations which are popular both at home and abroad. Indian cuisine too has its own fair share of well-loved, two dish combinations which can be served on their own as complete and wholesome meals. Some of these are listed on the next page, and all the recipes used are drawn from within the menus given in the previous pages.

Note : Accompaniment such as pickles, chutneys, paapads and simple salads may also be served if desired.

NON-VEGETARIAN TWO DISH MENUS

SEEKH KABAB AUR SHEERMAAL
Skewered mince meat kababs and rich, baked bread

TANDOORI MURGH AUR NAAN
Tandoori chicken and leavened, baked bread

CHAAP AUR TANDOORI ROTI
Lamb chops and grilled wholemeal bread

BHUNA KHEEMA AUR PURI
Minced meat curry and deep fried wholemeal bread

MUGHLAI KHORMA AUR PARATHA
Mughal-style lamb curry and shallow fried, unleavened bread

TAMATAR WALI MACHLI AUR PEELE ZEERE WALE CHAWAL
Tomato fish curry and yellow rice

DALCHA AUR BAGHARE CHAWAL
Split yellow peas with meat and seasoned rice

PRAWN VINDALOO AUR SADE CHAWAL
Hot and sour prawn curry and plain boiled rice

HYDERABADI BIRYANI AUR DAHI CHUTNEY
Chicken biryani and seasoned yoghurt

YAKHNI PULAO AUR KHEERE PYAZ KA RAITA
Lamb pulao with cucumber and onion yoghurt

VEGETARIAN TWO DISH MENUS

MILI JULI SABZION KA KHORMA AUR SHEERMAAL
Mixed vegetable curry and rich, baked bread

PALAK PANEER AUR NAAN
Home-made cheese with spinach curry and leavened, baked bread

KABULI CHANE AUR BHATURE
Dry spicy chick peas and deep fried leavened bread

ALOO TAMATAR KI TARKARI AUR PURI
Potatoes with tomato curry and deep-fried, wholemeal bread

MATAR PANEER AUR PARATHA
Home-made cheese with peas curry and shallow fried, unleavened bread

DHULI MOONG KI DAAL AUR PEELE ZEERE WALE CHAWAL
Split green beans and yellow rice

DUM ALOO AUR BAGHARE CHAWAL
Fried potatoes in spicy gravy and seasoned rice

RAJMAH AUR SADE CHAWAL
Curried red kidney beans and plain boiled rice

NAVRATAN BIRYANI AUR DAHI CHUTNEY
Mixed vegetable biryani and seasoned yoghurt

MATAR PULAO AUR ALOO KA RAITA
Rice pulao with peas and yoghurt with potatoes

LUNCH BOX MENUS

A lunch box in India is commonly called a 'tiffin' and tiffin time is always something to look forward to during the course of a long working day. With a little bit of thought and care, a delightful element of surprise can be maintained; for packed lunches can otherwise so easily get monotonous.

Listed on the next page are a few ideas for Indian style packed lunch boxes, using some of the recipes already given, which we are sure will provide a welcome variety and change. The ideal lunch box fare should be both tasty and nutritious. Try the following suggestions and you might surprise yourself! Do not forget to include a drink (e.g., tea, coffee, a yoghurt based drink or other drink) and some fresh fruit/salad in your lunch box (Try and avoid raw onions please!)

NON-VEGETARIAN	VEGETARIAN
1. PARATHA, SEEKH KABAB, CHUTNEY	1. PARATHA, ALOO TUK, ANY CHUTNEY
2. PURI, KHEEMA	2. PARATHA, SOOKHI KHUMBI
3. PURI, SHAAMI KABAB	3. PURI, ALOO TAMATAR KI TARKARI
4. BHATURE, CHICKEN TIKKA	4. PURI WITH CHAUNKI HUI MATAR
5. SHEERMAAL, KALEJI	5. BHATURA, CHANA
6. HYDERABADI BIRYANI (ONLY IF LEFT OVER!)	6. SHEERMAAL, TIKKI (MIXED VEGETABLE CUTLET)
7. SAMOSA (KHEEME KA), CHUTNEY	7. NAVRATAN BIRYANI, NATURAL YOGHURT
8. CURRY PUFFS, CHUTNEY	8. SAMOSA, CHUTNEY
9. TOASTED SANDWICH WITH ANY LEFTOVER DRY COOKED MEAT/ CHICKEN FILLING	9. TOASTED SANDWICH WITH ANY DRY COOKED VEGETABLE FILLING
10. SANDWICH WITH SHAAMI KABAB AND CHUTNEY	10. SANDWICH WITH CHEESE AND ANOKHI CHUTNEY

DIETING INDIAN STYLE – A Common Sense Approach

Food is at the heart of the traditions and culture of any society, particularly so in Indian society, where it is an inseparable part of the discipline of daily living—what with its numerous days of feasting and fasting! It is indeed commonly believed in India that with regards to food there are three types of people viz., yogi, bhogi and rogi.

Firstly, there is the "yogi" (one who is an ascetic) who is perfectly happy and content with the barest minimum of simple food. Then there is the "bhogi" (one who loves the pleasures of life, specially food), who eats not only to survive but also enjoys what he eats. Finally, there is the "rogi" (one who suffers from bad health) who not only loves food excessively, but is prone to suffer from ill-health due to his eating habits.

If this way of thinking is extended further to food lovers all over the world, the majority can be classed as "bhogis"! And, if we are honest with ourselves, don't many of us tend to overeat just because we love food so much? As a consequence, we gain unwanted weight, without even being aware of it.

It is not until our bodies in one way or the other begin to send us signals, do we decide to do something about our eating habits and excessive weight. Our first step is then to seek out that "miracle diet" which might hopefully restore our bodies to the shape we would like them to be. Our own experience has shown us that many a "miracle diet" which has been started with great enthusiasm falls flat as it is difficult to maintain a strict and demanding, often monotonous routine (Notwithstanding all the forbidden 'binges' in between!)

Contrary to many people's belief, dieting with Indian food is not only possible but is rewarding and exciting as well. Our diet plans with Indian food are an overall sound approach to sensible eating. They are based on the simple fact that we can help ourselves by reducing the "quantity" not "quality" of our required daily intake over a given period of time, and in that lies the key to success. We certainly make no claims to having all the answers to the vexed questions of dieting, nor are we dieticians who advocate the usual regimes of strict calorie counting. Common sense tells us that it is not only the individual foods that are the culprits, but what we eat over a period of time i.e., our eating habits, that really matter.

214

Never has there been more information available or greater awareness regarding nutrition and diet than there is now. But it has also left the average person somewhat nonplussed, for what the experts claim is good for us today could turn out to be bad for us tomorrow! We are also told that eating everything in moderation is fine, so why can't that be the best way forward?

A major obstacle to serious dieting is having to prepare separate meals for the individual on a diet as compared to the rest of the family and this gets more and more difficult to maintain as time goes on. Our diet plans draw upon an inexhaustible source of cooking inspirations which enables one to adapt day to day family meals to both the individual on diet and the family's requirements. A little bit of ingenuity allows the whole family to enjoy the same meal without necessarily sacrificing much of the recipe's original appeal.

Here are a few points which are essential to bear in mind while following our diet plan.

FATS

Reduce fat intake to a minimum.

When adapting any recipe reduce the fat content by at least half, or even omit it altogether where possible. This is easier with Indian cooking as much of the fat used is 'visible' rather than 'hidden'. Always skin poultry and use lean cuts of meats. Instead of ghee use vegetable oils such as corn oil or sunflower oil, and preferably use a non-stick pan.

SUGAR

Eliminate added sugar altogether as it provides no real nutrition whatsoever and is correctly described as a "sweet poison" by many an expert. However, natural sugar as found in fruit etc., is acceptable. In case of a sweet tooth use any of the multitudes of sugar substitutes available in the market.

SALT

Go easy on salt. Although it is important for taste, salt is known to be harmful when taken in excess.

PROTEINS

A must for everybody, they are necessary for growth and repair of body tissues. Various meats, dairy products, cereals, lentils and pulses are a good source of supply. Try to eat white meat e.g., chicken, fish, instead of red meats. Use skimmed or semi-skimmed milk and low fat yoghurts and cheeses instead of whole dairy produce.

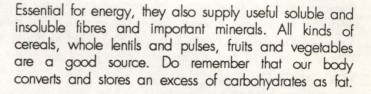

CARBOHYDRATES

Essential for energy, they also supply useful soluble and insoluble fibres and important minerals. All kinds of cereals, whole lentils and pulses, fruits and vegetables are a good source. Do remember that our body converts and stores an excess of carbohydrates as fat.

VITAMINS AND MINERALS

Needed in minute quantities, they are vital for the proper metabolism and working of the body. A varied and balanced diet will easily provide the necessary requirements. Overcooked and highly processed foods loose essential vitamins and minerals to some extent. Fresh and raw vegetables and fruits are recommended.

FLUIDS

Fluids are extremely important for the proper functioning of the body as they play an important role in helping to get rid of the various toxins and waste matter. Try and regularly drink 2 to 3 pints of water daily.

KNOW YOURSELF

Above all be kind to yourself. If hunger pangs strike in between meals, don't try and be a martyr! Go ahead, help yourself and eat something as long as it is some fresh fruit or raw vegetable, or have a low fat drink such as buttermilk, fruit juices, tea or coffee (sugarless). This will not only keep you in a cheerful state of mind, but will also prevent the tendency to overeat at the next meal.

PORTIONS

Try and consciously reduce the size of the portions of food that you eat daily and this will gradually re-educate the stomach to be satisfied with less. (Think of the "yogi"!) Make meal times regular and do not rush through your food, give yourself a chance to enjoy what is on your plate.

EXERCISE

We all realize that some form of regular exercise is important for general good health. It need not necessarily be strenuous but exercise we all must. Choose a form of exercise that you can maintain regularly and comfortably. A combination of regular exercise along with an awareness of proper eating habits is what every "body" needs!

The following diet programme has been worked out to help you to begin dieting with Indian food. Once you have tried it out and wish to pursue it further you will be able to adapt many recipes in this book with the help of the guidelines given above. We hope dieting with Indian food not only appeals to you but also leaves you with a sense of satisfaction and well-being.

SEVEN DAY DIET MENU
– for vegetarians

Suggested below is a diet plan for a week, which can be extended further in various permutations and combinations for as many days as required for successful dieting.

Essential points to remember

1. When adapting any recipe for the diet plan, reduce the quantity of oil/butter/ghee used by half or omit it entirely if possible.

2. When using yoghurt always use the low fat variety; and use semi-skimmed milk rather than ordinary full cream milk.

3. Instead of sugar use an artificial sweetener.

4. Tea/coffee with meals is optional, and may be substituted with plain water/unsweetened fruit juice. Remember to drink 4-6 glasses of water daily, either with or in between meals.

The fruits suggested below may be substituted with any other variety which is readily available. And remember, small to moderate portions only!

DAY 1

BREAKFAST

Annannas ka ras (Pineapple juice)
Dabal-roti aur shahad (Toast with a little honey)
Chai/Coffee (Tea/Coffee)

LUNCH

Chane aur lauki ki daal (Split yellow peas with white gourd)

Sada chawal (Plain boiled rice)
Mixed salad
Paapad (Dry roasted poppadum)
Papita (Slice of papaya/Paw-paw)
Chai/Coffee (Tea/Coffee)

DINNER

Namkeen nimbu paani (Savoury lime juice drink)
Palak aloo ki bhaji (Potatoes with spinach)
Tandoori roti (Grilled wholemeal unleavened bread)
Kheere ka raita (Low fat yoghurt with cucumber)
Aadoo (Fresh Peach)

DAY 2

BREAKFAST

Tarbooz (Piece of watermelon)
Dalia (A bowl of porridge)
Chai/Coffee (Tea/Coffee)

LUNCH

Toorai ka saalan (Courgette curry)
Chappati (Wholemeal unleavened bread)
Aloo ka raita (Low fat yoghurt with potatoes)
Amrood (Fresh guava)

DINNER

Tamatar ka ras (Tomato juice)
Lobhia (Black-eyed beans)
Hare dhanie ki chutney (Green coriander chutney)
Chai/Coffee (Tea/Coffee)

DAY 3

BREAKFAST

Missi roti (Lightly spiced, mixed-flours bread)
Dahi (Low fat natural yoghurt)
Chai/Coffee (Tea/Coffee)

LUNCH

Khatte chane (Chick pea curry)
Sada chawal (Parboiled rice)
Hara salaad (Green salad)
Lychees
Chai/Coffee (Tea/Coffee)

DINNER

Baingan ka bharta (Roasted aubergines)
Chappati (Wholemeal unleavened bread)
Mili juli sabzion ka achaar (Mixed vegetable pickle)
Dahi aur kela (Low fat yoghurt with bananas)

DAY 4

BREAKFAST

Tamatar ka ras (Tomato juice)
Bhuna bhutta (Roasted corn on the cob)
Chai/Coffee (Tea/Coffee)

LUNCH

Namkeen nimbu paani (Savoury lime juice drink)
Sookhi khumbi (Indian style garlic mushrooms)
Chappati (Wholemeal unleavened bread)
Aloo ka raita (Low fat yoghurt with potatoes)
Chai/Coffee (Tea/Coffee)
Annannas (Fresh pineapple)

DINNER

Tadke wali daal (Seasoned red lentils)
Sada chawal (Parboiled rice)
Baingan akhrot ka raita (Yoghurt with aubergines and walnuts)
Nimbu ka achaar (Lime pickle)
Aam (Fresh mango)

DAY 5

BREAKFAST

Santre ka ras (Orange juice)
Dahi aur kela (Low fat yoghurt with banana)
Chai/Coffee (Tea/Coffee)

LUNCH

Aloo tamatar ki tarkari (Potato and tomato curry)
Sada chawal 2 (Parboiled rice)
Paapad (Dry roasted poppadum)
Mixed salad
Chai/coffee (Tea/coffee)

DINNER

Chaunki hui matar (Lightly seasoned peas)
Tandoori roti (Grilled, wholemeal unleavened bread)
Lauki ka raita (Yoghurt with white gourd)
Khubani (Fresh apricots)

DAY 6

BREAKFAST

Chakotra (Fresh grapefruit)
Dalia (A bowl of porridge)
Chai/Coffee (Tea/Coffee)

LUNCH	Bharwi mirch (Stuffed green peppers) Chappati (Wholemeal unleavened bread) Kheere aur pyaz ka raita (Low fat yoghurt with cucumber and onion) Seb (Apple)
DINNER	Namkeen nimbu paani (Savoury fresh lime drink) Rajmah (Curried red kidney beans) Sada chawal 2 (Parboiled rice) Hara salaad (Green salad) Chai/Coffee (Tea/Coffee)

DAY 7

BREAKFAST	Lassi namkeen/mithi (Savoury/sweet buttermilk) Dabal-roti (Slice of toast) Chai/Coffee (Tea/Coffee)
LUNCH	Matar pulao (Rice with peas) Dahi chutney (Seasoned low fat yoghurt) Nashpati (Fresh pear)
DINNER	Palak paneer/Tofu (Home-made cheese and spinach curry) Naan (Baked, leavened bread) Sirke wale pyaz (Onion rings in vinegar) Chai/Coffee (Tea/Coffee)

SEVEN DAY DIET MENU
– for non-vegetarians

Suggested below is a diet plan for a week, which can be extended further in various permutations and combinations for as many days as required for successful dieting.

Essential points to remember
1. When adapting any recipe for the diet plan, reduce the quantity of oil/butter/ghee used by half or omit it entirely if possible.
2. When using yoghurt always use the low fat variety; and use semi-skimmed milk rather than ordinary full cream milk.
3. Instead of sugar use an artificial sweetener.
4. Tea/coffee with meals is optional, and may be substituted with plain water/unsweetened fruit juice. Remember to drink 4-6 glasses of water daily, either with or in between meals.

The fruits suggested below may be substituted with any other variety which is readily available. And remember, small to moderate portions only!

DAY 1

BREAKFAST

Tarbooz (Piece of watermelon)
Dabal-roti aur shahad (Toast with a little honey)
Chai/Coffee (Tea/Coffee)

LUNCH

Grilled chicken tikka
Chappati (Unleavened bread)

Mooli aur kheere ka salaad (White radish and cucumber salad)
Amrood (Guava)

DINNER

Murgh ka soup (Chicken soup)
Sada chawal (Parboiled rice)
Tamatar ki machli (Tomato fish)
Hara salaad (Green salad)
Coffee

DAY 2

BREAKFAST

Taza annannas (Slice of fresh pineapple)
Ubla anda (Boiled egg)
Chai/Coffee (Tea/Coffee)

LUNCH

Dalcha (Lamb cooked with lentils)
Sada chawal (Parboiled rice)
Mixed salad
Chai (Tea)

DINNER

Namkeen nimbu paani (Savoury lime juice drink)
Kaleji kabab (Liver kabab)
Tandoori roti (Grilled, unleavened wholemeal bread)
Kheere ka raita (Cucumber in seasoned yoghurt)
Papita (Slice of papaya)

DAY 3

BREAKFAST

Orange and pineapple juice
Bhuna bhutta (Roasted corn on the cob)
Chai/Coffee (Tea/Coffee)

LUNCH

Tabak maas (Lamb spare ribs)
Chappati (unleavened bread)
Hare dhanie ki chutney (Green coriander chutney)
Dahi aur kela (Low fat yoghurt with bananas)

DINNER

Namkeen lassi (Savoury buttermilk)
Boti kabab (Skewered pork kabab)
Sada chawal (Parboiled rice)
Aloo ka raita ((Potatoes in low fat natural yoghurt)
Chai (Tea)

DAY 4

BREAKFAST
Mithi lassi (Sweet buttermilk—with low fat sweetener)
Dabal-roti (Toast)
Chai/Coffee (Tea/Coffee)

LUNCH
Tandoori chicken (Spicy grilled/baked chicken)
Tandoori roti (Grilled wholemeal bread)
Hara Salad (Green salad)

DINNER
Mutton soup
Chilke wali moong ki khichdi (Rice cooked with lentils)
Sada dahi (Low-fat natural yoghurt)
Dolma nimbu ka achaar (pickled lime in lime juice)
Anaar (Pomegranate)

DAY 5

BREAKFAST
Tomato Juice
Anda (Poached or half boiled egg)
Tea/Coffee

LUNCH
Tandoori machli (Tandoori fish)
Chappati (Unleavened bread)
Dahi aur pudine ki chutney (Mint and low fat yoghurt chutney)
Chai (Tea)

DINNER
Namkeen lassi (Savoury buttermilk)
Tangri kabab (Grilled Chicken drumstick)
Sada chawal (Parboiled rice)
Kheere aur mooli ka salaad (Cucumber and white radish salad)
Coffee

DAY 6

BREAKFAST
Taza mausambi ka ras (Fresh grapefruit juice)
Dabal-roti (Toast)
Chai (Tea)

LUNCH
Seekh kabab (Minced lamb on skewers)
Aloo ka raita (Potato mixed in yoghurt)

Sada chawal (Parboiled rice)
Hare dhanie ki chutney (Green coriander chutney)
Chai (Tea)

DINNER
Nimbu paani (fresh lime drink)
Reshmi kabab (Chicken kabab)
Chappati (unleavened bread)
Mixed salad
Aam (Mango)

DAY 7

BREAKFAST
Santre ka ras (Fresh orange juice)
Dahi-kela (Banana in yoghurt)
Chai/Coffee (Tea/Coffee)

LUNCH
Shaami kabab (Lamb kabab)
Tandoori roti (Grilled wholemeal Bread)
Hara salad (Green salad)

DINNER
Chaap (Lamb chopps, grilled)
Moong ki khichdi (Rice cooked with moong beans)
Sirke wale pyaz (onion rings in vinegar)
Phalon ki chaat (Indian fruit salad)
Coffee

LIST OF INGREDIENTS USED

NAME OF INGREDIENT	INDIAN EQUIVALENT	COMMENTS
ALMOND	BADAAM	Although expensive, these nuts are widely used. They can be used either whole, powdered, or chopped—with or without skin.
ANISEED	SAUNF	Small, green, aromatic seeds of the anise plant. Used for flavouring food and drinks. Also used as an after dinner mouth freshener.
APPLE	SEB	Generally considered as one of the more expensive fruits in India. It is seldom used for cooking, other than for chutneys and jams.
APRICOT	KHUBANI	Found in greater abundance only in the cooler regions of India. It is sometimes used in cooking, in its dried form.
ASAFOETIDA	HING	A strong smelling resin gum with digestive properties. Used (particularly with lentils) in very minute quantities because of its overpowering flavour.
AUBERGINE	BAINGAN	Also known as brinjals. These glossy purple-skinned fruits of the egg-plant are an extremely common vegetable all over India. Grown in a profusion of shapes and sizes, they are cheaply available all year round. Choose firm, shiny brinjals without any blemishes.
BAKING POWDER	—	
BANANA	KELA	A very common fruit; banana flowers and raw green bananas may be cooked as vegetables, or the latter turned into chips. The large, shiny green leaves often find use as disposable plates.

NAME OF INGREDIENT	INDIAN EQUIVALENT	COMMENTS
BAY LEAF	TEJ PATTA	A herb which is mostly used whole in its dried leaf form for flavouring.
BLACK PEPPERCORNS	KALI MIRCH GOL MIRCH	These hot, black seeds can be used whole or powdered. Always use freshly milled pepper if powder is required.
BLACK SPLIT LENTILS	DHULI URAD KI DAAL	Creamy in taste when cooked. Soak for half an hour before cooking for best results.
BLACK WHOLE LENTILS	SAABUT URAD KI DAAL	Silky texture. Pre-soaking for 3-4 hours recommended as it takes a long time to cool and soften.
BREADCRUMBS	DABAL ROTI KA CHURA	
BUTTER	MAKHAN	
BUTTERBEANS		Large, flat, cream coloured beans, with a rich and velvety taste. Soak overnight.
BUTTERMILK	LASSI	A popular, thinned yoghurt drink, which is perhaps as old as Indian civilization itself! Now fast gaining popularity in the Western world.
CARDAMOM, BLACK	ILAICHI BADI/ MOTI	A relatively expensive and aromatic spice which is a native of India. The large, black variety has a more robust flavour and is an important ingredient of Garam Masala.
CARDAMOM GREEN	CHOTI/HARI ILLAICHI	The smaller, green variety which can be used along with its kin has a more delicate aroma, which makes it ideal for flavouring desserts.
CAROM	AJWAIN	These tiny seeds are used for seasoning; but should be used sparingly due to their strong and sharp flavour.
CARROT	GAJAR	
CAULIFLOWER	PHOOL GOBHI	
CAPSICUM	PHADI MIRCH/ SIMLA MIRCH	The green variety of capsicum is widely available in Indian markets, but the red and yellow variety is not as common. It is a delightful and colourful vegetable, ideal for salads, or combining with other vegetables and also used for stuffing with other ingredients.

227

"Who's Afraid of Indian Cooking?"

NAME OF INGREDIENT	INDIAN EQUIVALENT	COMMENTS
CHICK PEAS	KABULI CHANA	Creamish to pale golden in colour, they have a nutty and 'morish' taste. Soak overnight with a little bicarbonate of soda to enable them to soften and swell up.
CHICKEN	MURGH	Always skinned before use.
CHILLIES, GREEN	MIRCH, HARI	These fresh green chillies have a marvellous and delicate flavour, yet can be quite pungent in taste. Carefully scrape away seeds with a knife and discard, for a toned down effect. NOTE: DO NOT TOUCH EYES OR FACE whilst handling chillies! ALWAYS WASH HANDS immediately after handling chillies to avoid any discomfort.
CHILLIES RED, WHOLE	SABUT LAL MIRCH	A fiery spice used whole in its dried form for seasoning. A wide variety is available ranging in strength, but beware of the tiny, dark variety which is invariably a killer! NOTE: Take same PRECAUTION as with green chilies.
CHILLI POWDER	PISI LAL MIRCH	This is prepared by powdering the whole red chillies. It is exceedingly hot and should be used with caution. Use according to taste or even omit altogether if desired, as this is the main culprit which makes a dish 'hot' or 'fiery'. It is interesting to note that the entire economy of certain villages in Western India is tied up with the production and processing of red chilli powder.
CHILLI SAUCE		A Far Eastern condiment which has its uses in Indian cooking.
CINNAMON	DALCHINI OR DARCHINI	This is the inner tender bark of the cinnamon tree. Cinnamon can be used whole or powdered for flavouring.
CLOVES	LAUNG	An aromatic, dried flower bud possessing medicinal qualities. Used whole to enrich and flavour meat and rice or vegetable dishes or powdered and used as a component of Garam Masala.
COCHINEAL	LAL RANG (KHANE KA)	Red food colouring.
COCONUT	GARI, NARIYAL	A very versatile ingredient—the kernel of the coconut fruit. Can be used both in its fresh and dried forms for both sweet and savoury dishes. To choose a fresh coconut, select one that feels heavy for its size and shows no sign

228

NAME OF INGREDIENT	INDIAN EQUIVALENT	COMMENTS
		of any mould, especially near the 'eyes'. On shaking it you should be able to hear the liquid moving inside.
COFFEE	KAFFEE	Grown extensively in the coffee plantations of South India, where most households indulge in roasting their own coffee beans freshly everyday!
CORIANDER SEEDS	DHANIE KE BEEJ	Small round yellowish seeds of the aromatic herb called coriander. Very extensively used both whole and powdered.
CORIANDER LEAVES (GREEN)	DHANIE KE PATTE/ HARA DHANIA/ KOTHMIR	Beautifully fragrant green leaves of the coriander plant. Used in cooking and garnishing.
CORNFLOUR	ARROWROOT	Starchy powder used for thickening soups (but not curries). It finds limited use in Indian cooking.
COURGETTE	TOORAI	Certainly not considered an exciting vegetable by many in India due to its great abundance. However, it has a mild and pleasant flavour, cooks in minutes, and is easily digestible.
CREAM CHEESE	PANEER	Fresh home-made cream cheese.
CROUTONS	DABAL ROTI KE TALE, CHOTE TUKRE	Small pieces of sliced fried bread. Used for garnishing soups.
CUMIN (BLACK)	ZEERA (KALA) OR SHAHZEERA	Tiny black seeds of the cumin plant. Used for flavouring savoury dishes.
CUMIN (WHITE)	(SUFAID)	These off-white cumin seeds have a more robust and nutty flavour than black cumin. Can be used whole or in powdered form.
CURRANTS	MUNACCA	Dried grapes.
CURRY LEAVES	CURRY PATTA OR MITHI NEEM	Evergreen leaves of the Kariwepillai plant, possessing a powerful and pleasant aroma. Largely used for seasoning, especially in Southern India. Dried curry leaves may also be used.

NAME OF INGREDIENT	INDIAN EQUIVALENT	COMMENTS
DATES	KHAJOOR	Sweet fruit of the datepalm tree. Consumed fresh or dried.
DOUBLE CREAM	MOTHI MALAI	
EGG	ANDA	
FENUGREEK LEAVES	METHI KE PATTE	Aromatic leaves of a herb. May be used fresh or dried.
FENUGREEK SEEDS	MEETHI-KE-BEEJ	Small dried yellow seeds with a characteristic bitter taste. Their dormant flavour becomes more pronounced when fried for seasoning. Use very sparingly!
FENUGREEK LEAVES	MEETHI-KI-BHAJI	Fresh leaves of fenugreek.
FISH	MACHLI	
FLOUR, PLAIN	MAIDA	
FLOUR, WHOLEWHEAT	ATTA OR CHAPPATI FLOUR	Flour Atta or Chappatti. The most commonly used flour for making Indian breads. Often sieved before use, if a finer texture is desired.
FOOD COLOUR RED YELLOW	TOMATO COLOURING LAL PILA	Obtained both in powder or liquid form. These colours do not in any way affect the taste of any dish—only its appearance, and may be omitted if desired.
FRENCH BEANS	HARI PHALLI	Slim tender green beans.
GARAM MASALA	GARAM MASALA	A blend of various spices, usually ground. See explanation on page 6
GARLIC	LAHSUN	Pods which release a characteristic strong smell when peeled or chopped. Garlic is well known for it's medicinal properties. It is extensively used in Indian cooking. Will keep for several weeks if stored in a cool, dry place.
GHEE	GHEE	Fat made from clarified butter. A favourite
GHEE, PURE	ASLI, DESHI GHEE	medium for Indian cooking because of the individual and delicate flavour it imparts.

NAME OF INGREDIENT	INDIAN EQUIVALENT	COMMENTS
GINGELLY	*TIL*	A variety of sesame seeds—also used for pickling.
GINGER	*ADRAK*	Aromatic root mistakenly referred to as 'root' of a tropical plant. Fresh ginger can be stored in a cool, dry place for several weeks.
GINGER, DRIED	*SONTH*	Dried ginger can be used whole or powdered. Do not substitute it for fresh ginger as the flavour is quite different.
GOURD	*LAUKI*	Pale green vegetable belonging to the gourd family.
GRAM FLOUR	*BESAN*	Flour made from yellow split gram.
GRAPE	*ANGOOR*	
GREEN SPLIT LENTILS	*DHULI MOONG KI DAAL*	The outer green skins of split moong are removed to reveal the yellow lentils within. These cook quickly and do not need pre-soaking.
GUAVA	*AMROOD OR JAAM*	A delicious and highly fragrant fruit with a green or yellowish skin and creamy or pinkish flesh. Extremely rich in Vitamin C.
KIDNEY BEANS (RED)	*RAJMAH*	*See* red kidney beans.
LAMB	*BAKRE KA GOSHTH*	The most popular red meat used in Indian cooking.
LEMON	*PILA NIMBU*	Citrus fruit with a sharp and sour tangy taste.
LETTUCE	*SALAAD KE PATTE*	
LIME	*HARA KAGZI NIMBU*	Citrus fruit with a sour taste (milder than a lemon) and pleasant aroma.
LIVER	*KALEJI*	
LYCHEE	*LITCHEE*	Beautifully fragrant, sweet and fleshy fruit enclosed in a lovely pink outer shell. Peel off the shell and remove and discard the inner brown seed before eating the creamy flesh.

231

NAME OF INGREDIENT	INDIAN EQUIVALENT	COMMENTS
MANGO, FRESH	AAM, TAZA FRESH	Considered as King of Indian fruits.
MANGO PULP	AAM KA GUDA	Can be made from mangoes or bought tinned.
MANGO, RAW GREEN	KACHCHA AAM KACHCHI AMBI	Unripened sour fruit used for pickles and chutneys.
MANGO, DRY POWDERED	AMCHUR	Raw mangoes sun dried and powdered; has a sour taste.
MEAT	GOSHTH	
MEAT TENDERIZER		Salt with an added agent (papain) for making raw meat tender, prior to its cooking.
MILK	DOODH	
MILK, CONDENSED		
MILK, EVAPORATED		
MINT, FRESH	PUDINA	Common aromatic herb.
MINT, BOTTLED		Preserved mint leaves.
MOLASSES	GUR	Unrefined blocks of canesugar.
MUSHROOMS	KHUMBI	Edible fungi.
MUSTARD, SEEDS	RAI, OR SARSON	Small and dark reddish brown seeds used for seasoning and pickling. They have a sharp flavour.
MUSTARD OIL	SARSON KA TEL	Mainly used for pickling, though sometimes used as a cooking medium also. The raw oil has a strong pungent taste which alters dramatically for the better when heated strongly.
NIGELLA	KALONJI	Small, black, tear-shaped onion seeds. Used whole for flavouring fish, vegetables and certain naans.
NUTMEG	JAIPHAL	Dried kernel of the fruit from the Myristic tree. Nutmeg is always freshly grated and used as a spice.

NAME OF INGREDIENT	INDIAN EQUIVALENT	COMMENTS
OKRA	BHINDI	Considered 'exotic' in the West it is not an out of the ordinary vegetable in India. Has a uniquely delicious taste and texture.
ONIONS	PYAAZ	Indispensable in Indian cooking! (Though some extremely strict vegetarian sects make do without onions and garlic.)
ONIONS, BUTTON	CHOTI GOL PYAAZ	Used whole for salads, pickling and for cooking.
ONIONS, SPRING	HARA PYAAZ	Used in salads and in cooking.
ORANGE	SANTRA, NARANGI	
PAPAYA	PAPITA, PAPAI	Fruit of the papaya tree. The ripe fruit has a distinctive and delicious taste and flavour.
PAPAYA, RAW	KACHCHA PAPITA	Often peeled and ground and used very effectively as a meat tenderizer.
PAPRIKA		Powder made from dried sweet red pepper. Quite mild compared to red chilli powder. Has limited use in authentic Indian dishes, but may be part-substituted for chilli powder if required.
PEACHES	AADOO	
PEANUTS	MOONGPHALLI	
PEAR	NASHPATI	
PEAS, GREEN	MATAR	One of the better loved and extensively used vegetables.
PEPPERCORNS	KALI MIRCH OR GOL MIRCH	Whole, round, dried berries—which when powdered produce black pepper.
PINEAPPLE	ANNANNAS	
PISTACHIO	PISTA	Expensive but popular dry fruit; eaten on its own as well as used for garnishing.
PLUM	AALOO BOKHARA	

"Who's Afraid of Indian Cooking?"

NAME OF INGREDIENT	INDIAN EQUIVALENT	COMMENTS
POMEGRANATE	ANAAR	A delicious fruit with ruby red, edible seeds.
POMEGRANATE DRY SEEDS	ANAARDANA	Dried seeds of a small and sour variety of pomegranates used in cooking.
POPPADUMS	PAAPAD	Paper-thin savoury wafers made from lentil flour.
POPPY SEEDS	KHUS-KHUS	Tiny, round, off-white seeds of the poppy plant (not to be confused with the opium producing plant). Used as a thickening agent for gravies (sauces).
PORK	SHIKAR	Not a commonly consumed variety of meat in India due to religious and other restrictions.
POTATO	ALOO	
PRAWN	JHINGA	
PUFF PASTRY		
PUNCH	SHARBAT	A combination of various ingredients to produce a hot or a cold drink.
RADISH	MOOLI	Two common varieties—long white type and small red kind. Their crisp texture and nutty but slightly pungent flavour makes them a popular ingredient for salads.
RAISIN	MUNACCA	Dried grapes.
RED KIDNEY BEANS	RAJMAH	Attractive kidney-shaped, dark red beans, which have a superb taste. Definitely require overnight soaking and very thorough cooking.
RED SPLIT LENTILS	DHULI MASOOR KI DAAL	Commonly available, shiny salmon pink coloured lentils; do not need any pre-soaking and cook within minutes. They turn into a pale yellow colour on cooking.
RICE	CHAWAL	A staple foodgrain: numerous varieties available.
RICE, FLAKED	POHE, CHIDWA	Parboiled, flattened dried rice.
ROSE ESSENCE ROSE WATER	GULAB JAL	Colourless liquid, distilled from rose petals and used for flavouring desserts.

NAME OF INGREDIENT	INDIAN EQUIVALENT	COMMENTS
SAGO	SABUDANA	Starch obtained from the sago palm tree and shaped into tiny bead forms.
SAFFRON	KESAR, ZAFRAAN	Stigmas of a particular type of crocus which produce a yellow colour and a unique and delicate flavour. Although saffron is the most expensive of all spices it is well worth having.
SALT	NAMAK	
SALT, ROCK	KALA NAMAK	A dark, purplish coloured, sea salt with a strong aroma— to be used sparingly.
SEMOLINA	SOOJI	A product of wheat. Can be used for sweet and savoury dishes.
SESAME SEEDS	TIL	Tiny tear-shaped creamy white seeds, widely used in cooking.
SILVER LEAVES	CHANDI KE VARAK	Pure silver beaten into extremely thin and light sheets. Edible and decorative.
SODA BICARBONATE	KHANE WALA SODA	
SODA WATER	SODA PAANI	
SOYA SAUCE		Strictly speaking not an Indian ingredient, but is used on the odd occasion.
SPINACH	PALAK	Rich in iron.
SUGAR	CHINI,	Shakkar, SHAKAR
SUGAR, BROWN		
SUGAR, CASTOR	PISI HUI CHINI	
SUGAR CRYSTALLIZED	MISHRI	
SULTANAS	KISHMISH	Seedless dried green grapes.
SWEETCORN	BHUTTA	

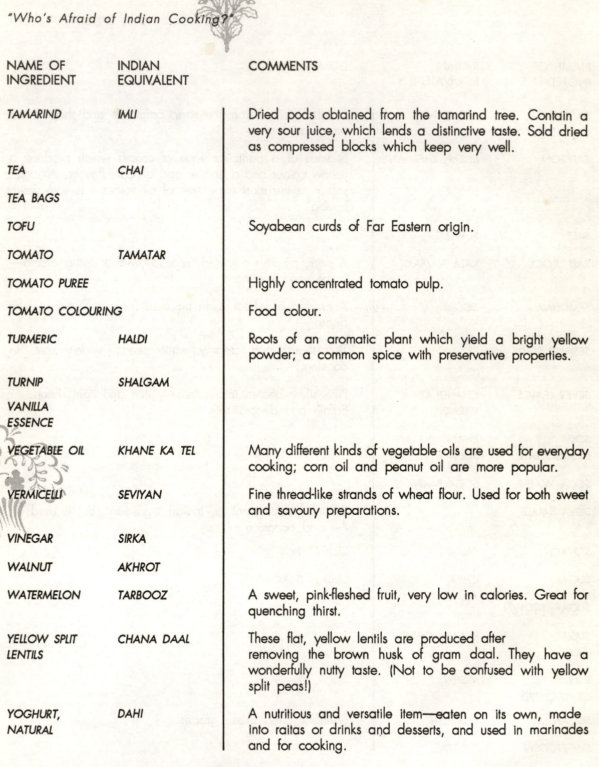

NAME OF INGREDIENT	INDIAN EQUIVALENT	COMMENTS
TAMARIND	IMLI	Dried pods obtained from the tamarind tree. Contain a very sour juice, which lends a distinctive taste. Sold dried as compressed blocks which keep very well.
TEA	CHAI	
TEA BAGS		
TOFU		Soyabean curds of Far Eastern origin.
TOMATO	TAMATAR	
TOMATO PUREE		Highly concentrated tomato pulp.
TOMATO COLOURING		Food colour.
TURMERIC	HALDI	Roots of an aromatic plant which yield a bright yellow powder; a common spice with preservative properties.
TURNIP	SHALGAM	
VANILLA ESSENCE		
VEGETABLE OIL	KHANE KA TEL	Many different kinds of vegetable oils are used for everyday cooking; corn oil and peanut oil are more popular.
VERMICELLI	SEVIYAN	Fine thread-like strands of wheat flour. Used for both sweet and savoury preparations.
VINEGAR	SIRKA	
WALNUT	AKHROT	
WATERMELON	TARBOOZ	A sweet, pink-fleshed fruit, very low in calories. Great for quenching thirst.
YELLOW SPLIT LENTILS	CHANA DAAL	These flat, yellow lentils are produced after removing the brown husk of gram daal. They have a wonderfully nutty taste. (Not to be confused with yellow split peas!)
YOGHURT, NATURAL	DAHI	A nutritious and versatile item—eaten on its own, made into raitas or drinks and desserts, and used in marinades and for cooking.